IN THE WAKE OF THE TANK.

IN THE
WAKE OF THE TANK

THE FIRST FIFTEEN YEARS OF MECHANIZATION IN THE BRITISH ARMY

BY

LIEUT.-COL. G. Le Q. MARTEL, D.S.O.,
M.C., R.E., M.I.Mech.E., p.s.c.

The Naval & Military Press Ltd

Published by

The Naval & Military Press Ltd
Unit 5 Riverside, Brambleside
Bellbrook Industrial Estate
Uckfield, East Sussex
TN22 1QQ England

Tel: +44 (0)1825 749494

www.naval-military-press.com
www.nmarchive.com

In reprinting in facsimile from the original, any imperfections are inevitably reproduced and the quality may fall short of modern type and cartographic standards.

CONTENTS.

CHAPTER.		PAGE.
I.	The Resuscitation of the Fighting Vehicle	1
II.	Tanks in 1917	14
III.	Tanks in 1918	29
IV.	Tank Characteristics and Experiments during the War	40
V.	The Tank as a Transport Vehicle	52
VI.	Tank Mechanical Engineering	58
VII.	Plans for 1919	69
VIII.	Experimental Work, 1919-21	80
IX.	Progress in Thought and Design, 1922-1926	91
X.	The Development of Cross-Country Transport	100
XI.	Small Tanks	110
XII.	The Passage of Tanks over Obstacles	123
XIII.	The Armoured Force on Salisbury Plain	147
XIV.	Anti-Tank Defence	170
XV.	The Mechanical Engineer in the Modern Army	180
XVI.	Present-Day Progress with Tanks	201
XVII.	Armoured Carriers and the Use of Unarmoured Vehicles	230
XVIII.	Conclusion	243

Appendix. Mechanical Details of Fighting Vehicles.

LIST OF PLATES.

		Facing Page
I.	Mark I Tank	4
II.	Medium "A" Tank (The Whippet)	24
III.	Mark V* Tank	26
IV.	Mark VIII. The Allied Tank	40
V.	Medium "C" Tank	42
VI.	Experimental Tank	86
VII.	The Snake Track	88
VIII.	Vickers Tank. Mark II	92
IX.	Dragon. Mark II	94
X.	Hathi Tractor. First Cross-Country Lorry	100
XI.	Crossley Half-Track Lorry	102
XII.	Morris Six-Wheel, 30-cwt. Lorry	104
XIII.	Overall Chain for Surmounting Obstacles	106
XIV.	The Original One-Man Tank	114
XV.	The Carden-Loyd Armoured Machine-Gun Carrier	122
XVI.	R.E. Tank, Carrying Bridge	132
XVII.	R.E. Tank, as Mine-Sweeper	132
XVIII.	R.E. Tool Lorry	138
XIX.	Pontoon Transport	140
XX.	Pontoon Bridge	142
XXI.	Tank Passing Over Stepping-Stones	144
XXII.	Light Box Girder Bridge	146
XXIII.	Heavy Tank (Experimental)	202
XXIV.	Medium Tank (Experimental)	204
XXV.	Light Tank (Experimental)	206
XXVI.	Lanchester Armoured Car	212
XXVII.	The Austin Scout	240

THE MARK V* TANK.

A typical type of heavy tank used by the British Army during the Great War. An unditching beam was carried on top of the tank.

The Lanchester Six-Wheel Armoured Car.

PREFACE.

The use of Tanks during the Great War led, quite naturally and logically, to the development of the use of the petrol engine and of cross-country traction for many purposes in the Army. The subject is now known as Mechanization, and is one in which great interest has been taken, not only in the Army, but by a large body of civilians as well. This interest was roused mainly by Major-General J. F. C. Fuller, who wrote profusely and in a most attractive manner on the subject for many years after the War. Our army to-day is ahead of all other nations in this direction; and is filled with zeal and a desire to forge ahead in this and other ways, in a manner which is without parallel in the history of post-war armies. This is due both to General Fuller's writings and to the exceptional activity of many of the authorities in the army during recent years, and very material progress has been made.

The early days of mechanization consisted solely of the use of tanks in trench warfare, and has been fully recorded in the war books on tanks. Other books have been written more recently on the trend of thought in mechanization since the war, but no consecutive history has been written showing the growth and development of this subject in the British Army—both mechanically and tactically—up to the present time.

It is with a view to filling the demand which is

believed to exist for a survey of this progress, from the arrival of the tanks to the present day, that this book has been written.

The development of the mechanical side and the tactical employment of machines must, necessarily, go hand in hand, and they are, therefore, described in stages—sometimes mixed and sometimes in separate chapters. This may appear a little confusing, but so closely are they connected that it was found even more confusing to try and separate them entirely.

It may be of interest to readers to notice how often ideas and proposals of the earlier days come up again for consideration and trial at a later stage. In fact, the whole of the work is of such a recent date that this will be constantly recurring, and no one can consider himself fully equipped to deal with the subject of mechanization who has not studied the ways and stages by which it has progressed in the recent past.

The first six chapters dealing with the period of the Great War have purposely been kept very short, as this work has already been so fully reported in other war books. The contents of these chapters have, therefore, been confined to an outline history and an attempt to bring out the main lessons from the war which can, perhaps, be more clearly seen at this time than when most of the war books were written.

My apologies are due for the many omissions of names and deeds in this brief account of the war period, but this was unavoidable.

It is hoped that the book as a whole gives a true account of thoughts and actions as they occurred. Present-day policy is now no longer a matter for individual ideas, and official manuals exist; but though these give guidance, they very wisely leave plenty of latitude, and new ideas are encouraged. In describing the thoughts and ideas of the present, it is hoped that the conflicting views are fairly stated, and that the book steers a reasonable middle course among them.

I have found it impossible to avoid describing my own personal work in places, and my excuse for this is that though I only played a small part, at any rate in the early days, I happened to be very closely connected with the movement from the start, and served on the General Staff, and also worked both as a Mechanical Engineer on the machines and as a Field Engineer with bridges for tanks.

Critics may object that the book is in the nature of an advertisement for the Army. Though the various mistakes that we have made are fairly described, the book certainly emphasises the great progress that has been made. I will make no excuses for this. Not only is it pleasing to be able to write and read about a subject in these days in which we are still ahead of other nations, but it is very desirable that the public should know about it. Being one of the oldest conservative bodies in the nation, the army has always abhorred anything in the nature of advertisement. Times, however, are changing, and the people demand as a right that they shall know what the army is doing and that their money is not being wasted. At present books are constantly appearing, stressing our mistakes and running us down, and until we let the public know through the Press that the whole truth is quite different to this, we shall continue to remain in the minds of the people as an old-fashioned body that objects to progress and is tied down by an out-of-date type of discipline and conventions.

Many soldiers would like to see more of our Military writers carrying out the necessary counter-propaganda to let the public know the truth and to enable them to realize what the army is doing, and, generally speaking, the efficient manner in which it is carried out.

It is hoped that this book may show them one direction in which the army is forging ahead on most efficient and up-to-date lines.

CHAPTER I.

THE RESUSCITATION OF THE FIGHTING VEHICLE.

THAT fighting vehicles of different types have been used at various stages in the history of war from the earliest days is known to any student of war; their existence was, however, invariably short lived, owing to the fact that they could never carry sufficient armour to keep out the missiles of the day. The propulsion of these vehicles was limited to man and horse power, and with this means they could not propel them if they carried the necessary weight of armour; hence, although they had occasional successes by the use of surprise, they lost all value as soon as it was discovered that the normal weapons of the fighting soldier, such as the archer's bow or the infantryman's musket, could pierce the armour with their missiles. It was not a case—as it is to-day—of the vehicle being proof against normal weapons and needing a special and somewhat heavy weapon to pierce the armour; had this been the case it is probable that we should have heard a great deal more about fighting vehicles in the past. The limited means of propulsion of these vehicles was still further reduced by the well-known limitations of wheeled vehicles when used off roads. If the endless track had been invented earlier, even the feeble muscular power of man and horse might have been found sufficient to drive a fighting vehicle cross country carrying sufficient armour to be proof against the lighter missiles. As it was, we had to wait for the development of both the internal combustion engine and the chain track before we were in a position to construct a fighting vehicle which could resist the effect of the normal weapons carried by the infantry.

This occurred at a time—some 20 years ago—when fighting vehicles had long since fallen out of use and been forgotten. Thus, although some engineers and inventors produced designs a few years before the Great War, and even made models of fighting vehicles using the chain track and the petrol engine, they were ignored by the military authorities of the day, who considered that they would easily be destroyed by shell fire. It is here that we get our first lesson in the study of the development of fighting machines. The lesson is not that all inventions should be more carefully studied by military men with a view to their employment in war, but that the military authorities should have a very clear idea of the main problems that will confront them in the next war and should, therefore, know the type of invention which they need to solve their problems. In this case the problem was not difficult to isolate.

The lessons from the Russo-Japanese War had brought out very clearly the great defensive power of the concealed machine gun, especially when protected by barbed wire. Several officers must have appreciated this as the main problem of the next war. There is at least one clear instance.

Major-General J. F. C. Fuller (then Captain Fuller), while a student at the Staff College at Camberley, in 1914 wrote a paper which brought this out quite clearly. He pointed out that long lines of trenches and machine guns were almost bound to occur in the next war, protected by wire entanglements, and the whole problem would be one of how to attack these lines. The only known solution was a very large increase in the volume of artillery fire, and he suggested that it was most urgent to increase our artillery to meet this demand which was bound to arise.

If this question had been more thoroughly discussed, it is reasonably certain that the difficulty of overcoming the concealed machine gun would have been accepted as the main problem of the next war. The solution of the problem should then have been kept in mind by the military authorities, and if this had been done there is every probability that they would have realised the great possibilities of reintroducing the fighting vehicle in its modern form when, on various occasions before the Great War, these suggestions and drawings were placed before them. There would then have been nothing to prevent them from secretly constructing the tank in the form in which it eventually appeared. If this experimental work had been carried out in peace time, before the war, we would have been in a position to produce large numbers of tanks at least a year sooner than they eventually appeared, and this might easily have affected the whole course of the war. Thus for a few thousand pounds spent as a wise insurance in peace time we might have been prepared, if the main problems of the war had turned out to be of the nature which we had anticipated, and millions in money and lives might have been saved.

We are in a much better position to-day. Various Boards and Committees examine all suggestions and inventions, but the true lesson from the pre-war days is not so much the necessity for the thorough consideration of these suggestions as the necessity for a clear conception by the General Staff of the main problems which are awaiting solution.

To-day we are in a position to compete with the concealed machine gun by using tanks; what, then, will be the main problem of the next great war if we should be forced into one by the terms of the Locarno Pact? Among the many possible answers to this question, there is the reply that just as infantry were unable to advance against the concealed machine gun in the last war, so the tank, when used in co-operation with an infantry attack, may be unable to advance against the concealed anti-tank gun. This may, or may not, prove to be one of the main problems of the next war, but the more we can debate and clear our minds on such points the easier will it be for us to guide the policy and direct the progress that we are making to-day in mechanization.

Although we missed a great opportunity of being ahead of all other nations, by having the antidote to the machine gun prepared in secret before the war, we were the first to make use of modern inventions, and evolve the tank when the necessity arose towards the end of 1914. It would be neither profitable, nor would there be space in this book to enter into details as regards the individual responsibility for the production of the tank. For the early prevision of the necessity and possibility of resuscitating the fighting vehicle, using the petrol engine and the track, the credit lies mainly with General Sir E. D. Swinton (then Lt.-Col. Swinton), who pressed for this as early as October, 1914. After many difficulties the necessary experimental work was carried out, being very materially assisted by Mr. Winston Churchill, who was then the First Lord of the Admiralty; and in February, 1915, the Mark I tank passed all its tests in a trial at Hatfield. An order was placed for the construction of 100 tanks, and a tank supply committee was formed under the Ministry of Munitions, with Major (later Sir) Albert Stern as chairman. Later, the number of tanks under construction was increased to 150. Details and characteristics of this Mark I tank are given in an appendix at the end of the book, and only a brief description need be given here. There were two types of tank—Male and Female. The only difference was in the sponsons* which carried the armament on each side of the tank. It was not possible to provide all-round fire in these sponsons for both a 6-pr. gun and a machine gun. Hence,

---

* A sponson is a naval term meaning a projecting turret on the side of a ship.

half the tanks—which were called male tanks—were equipped with a gun in each sponson, and the remainder were female tanks, with two machine guns in each sponson. The Mark I tank had a maximum speed on good ground of five miles an hour, could cross a clear gap of 10 feet, and climb a slope of 40 degrees.

In March, 1916, a unit was formed under the command of Col. Swinton to man the tanks which were under construction. The unit was composed of six companies, each of which was to have 25 tanks. For the purpose of secrecy it was named the Heavy Section Machine Gun Corps, and later this was changed to Heavy Branch M.G.C.

In spite of many difficulties and some opposition the unit was raised rapidly, and was full of zeal. The necessity for secrecy was personally impressed on all ranks by their Commander, and was religiously kept. By August two Companies were fully equipped and trained, and more tanks were arriving from the makers. The raising of this unit and their enthusiasm, and the way in which they guarded the secret was a great tribute to their Commander. It was at this stage that I first came in contact with tanks. In June, 1916, I was sent home from France to construct a typical trench warfare battlefield at Elverdon, in Norfolk, on which the tanks might practise. This was completed in a month, and I returned to the command of my Field Company in the 4th Division in time for the Somme offensive on July 1st.

In February, 1916, Colonel Swinton wrote his

proposals for the tactical employment of tanks. They proved to be a striking forecast of the correct method of using tanks, and had a very marked similarity to their actual employment as used at the battle of Cambrai in 1917. Briefly, the proposals were that tanks should not be used till large numbers were available, and that they should then be employed as a complete surprise on a wide front, and that the ground selected should be suitable to the limitations of tanks. A long extract from this remarkable paper appears in Colonel Fuller's book, "Tanks in the Great War," which also contains a much more detailed account of the various stages which led to the production of these Mark I tanks and the units which were to fight them.

Whether tanks could have been successfully launched in this way without preliminary tests on the battlefield we will discuss later, but the fact remains that no attention was paid to these views, and at the end of August, 1916, the first two Companies, with 50 tanks, were sent to France and used in an attack on September 15th, on the Somme. The ground was shell-torn anl cratered, and unsuitable for the use of tanks, and the machines themselves were used in driblets on a wide front. The result was a failure, from a tank point of view, most of them being unable to negotiate the ground.

A second attack took place on September 25th and 26th, in which 13 tanks were engaged, but the result was much the same. Nevertheless, a small number of tanks succeeded in crossing this shell-torn battlefield and gave very valuable assistance to the infantry in individual cases. As a result, it was decided to expand the arm to 1,000 tanks, which were to be ready for a great offensive in the spring of 1917. But the secret had been given away, and although the tanks had shown that they were a complete answer to the machine gun so long as the ground selected for the battle was within their capability, it was impossible to say whether they would be in the same position next spring, when the enemy had had some seven months in which to prepare a system of anti-tank defence.

This brings us to the second main lesson from the use of tanks during the Great War, namely, the question of the premature use of a small number of tanks, and it is one which has been much debated. Many reasons and excuses have been produced in defence of their early employment in this way. Some of them have been patched up out of loyalty to our great Commander during the War —Douglas Haig. No one who served at G.H.Q. during the war, or who saw the responsibilities which were cheerfully borne by Douglas Haig under the most trying circumstances, can express anything but the highest praise for his capabilities as a Commander. He has often been criticised by politicians and civilians, and this very point of the premature use of tanks has been used as an example of his inability. Yet within a few years of the conclusion of the war one finds politicians showing a weak, vacillating leadership every time any crisis arose which would have been incomprehensible to the Commander-in-Chief at G.H.Q. Just imagine what might have happened if Douglas Haig had been a weak man of this nature. In point of fact, he made up his mind—after mature consideration—that the war would be won on the Western Front. For two years he met failure after failure, but in spite of this and the constant proposals by the leading politicians that his forces should be dispersed in other directions, he remained calm and confident. This confidence outlasted the almost overwhelming attacks by the Germans in 1918, and led to the final and great victories on the Western Front which ended the war.

This diversion on the subject of the leadership of our Commander-in-Chief during the war is made because it is proposed to endeavour to deduce lessons and learn from our mistakes in the use of tanks during the war, and it might otherwise appear that I was presuming to deprecate the leadership of a man who proved himself to be the greatest man in the British Empire during those fateful days. That mistakes should be made was, however, inevitable, and it is now proposed to discuss whether this premature use of tanks was one of them.

This small batch of tanks was used in September, 1916, to resuscitate a failing offensive. In this they had little effect, and those who support the early use of a few tanks lay no claim to this as a suitable reason or excuse for doing so. Instead, the holders of this policy produce a threefold claim that a preliminary test on the battlefield was necessary for the successful development and use of tanks. Firstly, they state that the correct mechanical design of tanks and their proper tactical employment could not have been achieved without this preliminary test. Secondly, they claim that no Commander would have been justified in staking the whole success of a great offensive on the power of a machine to roll down the wire and silence the foremost machine guns without a trial in battle. Thirdly, they claim that no Government would have allowed the Ministry of Munitions to use the limited resources of manufacture and steel supply on the production of large numbers of untried fighting machines. The first of these claims is easily dealt with. As regards mechanical design, the Mark I tank only differed materially from the Mark IV tank, that was used so successfully in the battle of Cambrai, in that the latter had armour, proof against armour piercing bullets, and had track rollers which had been strengthened to stand the pavé roads of France. The Mark I tanks had a tail with wheels, which was a distinct asset to the tank in steering and negotiating wide trenches, but proved to be so liable to damage in battle that it was eliminated as an unnecessary expense in later models. As regards the thickness of armour, Col. Swinton deliberately chose an armour, proof only against ordinary small-arm ammunition for the Mark I tank, because he counted on a sufficient degree of surprise to ensure that the enemy was not prepared with unlimited supplies of armour-piercing ammunition, and in this he proved correct.

As a result the Mark I tank was handier than the later Marks of this type, due to having a reduced total weight. Thus we see that no material lesson was learnt from this early employment of a small number of tanks as regard their mechanical design. The minor alterations which were incorporated in the Mark IV tank would all have come to light with a little more training behind the front.

As regards their tactical employment, this was so obviously wrong in September, 1916, and the original proposals by Col. Swinton proved to be so eminently sound when tried at Cambrai in 1917, that no claim can be made that any tactical lessons were learnt in this first trial.

As regards the claim that no Commander would have been justified in risking the use of these machines in the manner proposed by Col. Swinton without a preliminary trial, this is, of course, purely a matter of opinion. Such risks have been taken in the past with overwhelming success, and it is now tolerably certain that a great success would have been attained if the risk had been taken in this case. Possibly the duration of the war might have been shortened by over a year.

Finally, we come to the last point, namely, the question as to whether the Ministry of Munitions would have produced the tanks. On this point there can really be little doubt. Mr. Lloyd George was Minister of Munitions at that time, and whatever his faults may be, he never lacked vision or courage. With a little support from military opinion he would certainly have diverted the necessary labour and steel from other activities for the production of the necessary tanks without a preliminary trial on the battlefield.

It is curious that few people have stressed the difficulty of effecting surprise in the debates on this point. Perhaps the overwhelming success of Col. Swinton in guarding the secret has silenced the critics. Yet even if we had waited till we had large numbers of tanks and had lost the secret by training the infantry with tanks for a few weeks prior to their employment in a great offensive, what could the Germans have done? One cannot produce anti-tank defence for a front which is 300 miles long in a few weeks, and we could still have kept the secret as to what part of the front was to be attacked. The result would have been the same, namely, a great initial success, such as the Cambrai battle, but perhaps on a wider front and backed up by large reserves instead of the feeble follow up which we saw at Cambrai.

Thus the lesson is that if a Commander sees an invention or new weapon which strikes at the root of his main problem and difficulties he is justified in taking the risk and employing it as a surprise and banking on it.

We are an inventive nation, and the opportunity will be offered again and again in the future. Let us hope that we have learnt our lesson from this example. The same does not quite apply in peace, because weapons with which troops are armed in peace cannot be kept secret, but the nation which forges ahead in this direction and produces the most modern weapons will always be slightly ahead of other nations, and—more important still—should have secret experimental work in hand in peace which will enable that nation to go right ahead and surprise the enemy shortly after the war has started with weapons which are a long way in advance of those possessed by other nations.

CHAPTER II.

TANKS IN 1917.

AFTER the employment of tanks in September, 1916, the Heavy Branch Machine Gun Corps, as we were then called, was reorganized on a proper basis in France. Colonel H. J. Elles (now Major-General Sir H. J. Elles) was appointed to command, with myself as Brigade Major, Captain T. J. Uzielli as D.A.A. and Q.M.G., and Captain F. E. Hotblack was Intelligence Officer. Colonel Uzielli remained at the head of the administrative side throughout the war, and a large share of our success was due to his work, and Lt.-Colonel Hotblack's work for the Corps is too well known to need any further mention. Throughout the war we were an active Headquarters, and few actions took place without some member of our Staff being present to see what was happening. In this way our Commander (who also usually went up to see things for himself) was kept closely in touch with the situation. During a pause in a battle we would take the opportunity of talking to Section and Company Commanders and learn their difficulties, and a very good feeling grew up between units and Headquarters.

The existing companies were formed into four tank battalions. Each battalion was to consist of three companies, and each company of four sections. The section was to consist of five tanks, but this was later reduced to four, so that the battalion possessed 48 tanks. We settled down at once to training in an area round our Headquarters at Bermicourt, near St. Pol, and made preparations to take part in the offensives in the spring and summer of 1917. In order to clear our minds as to the possible eventual future of tanks, we prepared a paper which was called " The Tank Army," in November, 1916. Though not of any special value, the paper raised considerable interest at the time, and I still have a copy. It is probably the first paper ever written suggesting the employment of an army consisting entirely of fighting vehicles, and it is mentioned here to show that we were thinking on these lines even in those early days, before any tank had travelled at more than a few miles an hour. The paper suggested strongly defended tank bases from which the tank armies would emerge for war. They would be led by fast tanks capable of moving at 20 miles an hour, and backed up by heavier and more powerful tanks moving up more slowly in rear. Sappers and Signals were to be in tanks to accompany the fighting tanks, and both medical anl workshop assistance accompanied them in tanks. All tanks were to be made to swim to overcome the restraining influence of rivers and canals (this was achieved in 1919 with an experimental tank). Tank bases were to be heavily defended with mines and obstacles against raids by enemy tanks, and supplies were to be convoyed by fighting tanks. In

December, 1916, I discussed this paper with Colonel J. F. C. Fuller, who had just arrived at H.Q. Tank Corps as G.S.O.I., while I became G.S.O.H. to the Corps. It was a crude paper, and after a short time Colonel Fuller relieved me of any work of this nature by writing about the great future possibilities of tanks in a manner which eventually raised the widest interest.

The most urgent question at this time was the design and construction of the new tanks. There were 70 Mark I tanks in France and some Mark II and III tanks were due to arrive later with some very minor improvements.

Everything now hinged on the question of tank design. As the secret had been exposed it was obvious that the armour must be made proof against armour-piercing bullets. This presented no great difficulty other than a slight loss in handiness in the tank due to the increased weight. There were also other defects in the Mark I. These were due to the difficulties under which the tank was produced, and were obvious from the start. They were in no way lessons produced from the premature use of tanks. Other than the undesirability of fitting a tail, which has already been mentioned, the main points were the necessity for one man control in the tank and some arrangements to simplify the fitting of the sponsons on the tank. The Mark I tank was controlled by three men, one of whom had to work secondary gears at the rear of the machine for steering and changing speed, under orders from the driver in front. This was obviously undesirable, and had only been permitted in the Mark I tank owing to the difficulty of getting suitable gears and controls tested and made in time. As regards the sponsons, the Mark I tanks had to remove the gun sponsons for travel by rail, and this meant man-handling a very heavy weight and moving it on a trolley—a most tedious operation. Later, a method was devised of folding the sponson inside the tank, which saved all this serious delay when entraining or detraining and preparing for action. The Tank Supply Committee, under the able chairmanship of Colonel Stern, were quite alive to these points, and in November, 1916, they offered a new design of tank, which, though very similar to the Mark I tank in appearance, possessed an excellent system of one man control and incorporated all the above points. This proposed tank was very similar to the eventual Mark V tank, and if the authorities had agreed to the design, large numbers of these machines would have been available by the spring of 1917. It was, however, a matter for decision by the General Staff at the War Office and G.H.Q., and they were faced by a difficult question. Would the original idea of an attack on a wide front as a surprise with tanks now be possible? The secret was given away, and the Germans had many months in which to prepare an anti-tank defence scheme. If it was possible, then what we wanted were large numbers of these slightly improved tanks as early as possible. If, however, anti-tank arrangements had become a serious factor, such, for instance, as continuous minefields in or behind the barbed wire defences, then we needed a tank whose main object would be to assist the infantry in mopping up in a battle of the "Somme" type. For this purpose, a tank which could negotiate a shell-torn battlefield was needed, and for this it was suggested that we would need an entirely new design of tank, with perhaps three or more tracks, or much wider tracks. This meant a great delay, due to the necessary experimental work; but if this was what was required, it was better to wait than to produce useless tanks of the existing type. There was, of course, much discussion on this problem, and time was passing rapidly. No decision was reached by the end of 1916, and by that time the only possibility left, if tanks were required for the following summer, was the production of what became known as the Mark IV tank. As already stated, this was very similar to the Mark I tank, but the sponson difficulty and other minor defects had been put right and the armour was proof against armour-piercing bullets. Owing to the delay, it was not possible to incorporate the new epicyclic gears giving one-man control, which had been designed by Lt.-Col. Wilson, at the Ministry of Munitions, towards the end of 1916.

This was a great lesson to the General Staff. Soldiers are used to making quick decisions in tactical, and even strategical problems; to this they must now add quick decisions as regards the mechanical design of their weapons, and this point will be referred to later. Lt.-Col. Stern, as Chairman of the Supply Committee, was very justly angry at what he considered the intolerable delay in the decision over this matter.

In the meantime, Cól. Swinton was raising new units in England and furthering the tank movement at home. Although he had initiated and raised the Corps, Col. Swinton was quite content that it should be commanded in France by Col. Elles, while he directed operations at home under the War Office. But in March, 1917, General Anley was appointed to this position. When we remember that Col. Swinton had gained intimate experience and knowledge in raising and launching the whole scheme, it is no reflection on his successor to point out that Col. Swinton's loss was a great blow to the Tank Corps, and cost us dearly.

In May, 1917, Major-General Capper was appointed to succeed General Anley, and became Chairman of the Tank Committee at home. This did much to assist our Corps in France.

The time for spring and summer offensives was now approaching, and it was decided that the tanks were again to be used in sections to mop up for the infantry and not to lead a surprise attack on a wide front, which was ever the hope and wish of our Corps.

At Arras, in April, 1917, 60 tanks were used to mop up for the infantry, and were useful in a few cases. But they were Mark I and II tanks, and were not bullet-proof, and suffered many casualties from armour-piercing bullets. Thus we found that the Germans had anticipated a renewal of tank attacks, and had provided their machine-gunners with unlimited armour-piercing ammunition; but other than this he had made no special preparations for anti-tank defence. If, therefore, the authorities had taken the risk and made large numbers of improved Mark I tanks (with thicker armour) without delay, the original proposal of a surprise attack with tanks crushing the wire and subduing the machine-guns on a wide front could have been successfully launched in the spring of 1917.

As it was, we made little headway. Messines was an artillery battle, with no scope for tanks at all. Ypres, in August, 1917, was a ghastly failure, from a tank point of view. Before the eight days' preliminary bombardment for the battle had started the ground was comparatively dry, and although this low-lying land was not the most suitable for tanks, yet it is reasonably certain that a surprise attack could have been launched with only a very short preliminary bombardment of a few minutes, and that the tanks would have led the infantry successfully on to the Passchendaele ridge on the first day of the attack. This proposal was made by the Tank Corps (we had been re-named the Tank Corps in July, 1917); but against this was set the great success of Messines as an artillery battle. Those responsible for the third battle of Ypres argued that while they had the recent example of a great success at Messines by making full use of our superior artillery, why should they risk a novel method of attack involving considerable risk. The answer to this (though it is being wise after the event) is that an enemy is rarely caught napping twice running by the same trick, and that surprise is essential in war. In this case the Germans withdrew their troops for the bombardment and counter-attacked our troops as they were endeavouring to cross the sodden shell-torn ground which our bombardment had produced. With the ground in this condition our tanks were practically useless, though as usual there were individual instances where they gave great assistance to the infantry and arrived at their objective after the most heroic efforts on the part of the crews.

This failure of the tanks during 1917 had, however, one beneficial result, though it was quite unintentional on our part. The Germans formed the opinion that tanks were quite useless, and incidentally, many British officers formed the same view. This made it possible for us still to use the tanks in the manner which Col. Swinton had originally proposed, because the Germans had paid little attention to anti-tank defence. This project was continually in our minds at H.Q. Tank Corps, and at last we were given our chance at the battle of Cambrai, in November, 1917.

This battle has been so fully reported in other books that only a brief reference is needed here. The tank used was the Mark IV, with its clumsy system of control, and 378 tanks were available. The advance, which took place on an eight-mile front, penetrated to a depth of 10,000 yards in 12 hours, and over 8,000 prisoners and 100 guns were captured. The attack was not preceded by any preliminary bombardment, and came as a complete surprise to the enemy. The tanks crushed lanes through the uncut wire and subdued the dreaded machine-guns, enabling the infantry to advance with insignificant casualties. This action reintroduced the essential element of surprise in battles on the Western Front, and probably gave the Germans the idea of using only a short, sudden bombardment before launching their assault in their offensive in March, 1918. By this time trenches had grown to a great width on this part of the front, and a detailed investigation before the battle showed that the Mark IV tank could not span the widest trenches. A large fascine was, therefore, carried by every tank and dropped into the trenches to form crossing places. This incident is mentioned because it shows how a known obstacle can be surmounted by mechanical means; provided the nature of the obstacle is known beforehand, it is usually possible to contrive some method of overcoming it, and other instances of this nature will be referred to later; it is the unknown obstacle, such as a concealed minefield, that becomes the real threat to tanks.

The battle was an overwhelming success. Led by our commander, General H. J. Elles, in the leading tank of the centre brigade, the tanks went from objective to objective. General Elles, in whom the whole Tank Corps had complete trust, had always been a firm believer in the original proposals that tanks should be used in this way, and now our claims were justified. There were, however, critics who stated that no great advantage was gained; no break-through followed, and that such an operation could never be repeated with success. They even blamed the tanks when we continued to sit in the salient we had made, and were eventually driven out by a counter-attack. Their views were without foundation. The battle occurred at a time when our reserves had all been exhausted in the third battle of Ypres; and although we might have done more than we did, there were no suitable forces available to follow up a success of this nature, and if none could be made available we should have withdrawn from the extremities of the salient that we had made; it was no fault of the tanks that we did not do so.

This question of exploitation after the break-through raised a new and important point. It had always been thought that if the tanks put the infantry through the main trench system, the latter would be able to advance in the mobile warfare beyond without assistance from the tanks. It has already been stated that few troops were available for this purpose, and the cavalry were late in arriving; and it could not, therefore, be considered a test case; but such troops as did pass through were held up comparatively easily by machine-guns that had been rushed up for this purpose. All our tanks had been used up in the assault, and even if more had been available their limited speed and circuit of action rendered them unsuitable for rapid break-through operations of this nature. We had always had in mind the necessity for a number of tank units equipped with faster machines; in fact, our projected expansion had included a number of these units, but we now had definite proof that faster machines, with a longer circuit of action, were necessary for this semi-mobile warfare beyond the main trench systems.

This had already been foreseen by the Tank Supply Department at home, and the first of these Medium Tanks—the Medium A, or Whippet, as it was called—had been designed by Mr. W. Tritton (later Sir William Tritton) as early as December, 1916. The first tanks of this type reached France soon after the battle of Cambrai. At this time a certain nomenclature for tanks had been decided on, and as the nomenclature is the same to-day, it is worth recording. Tanks were divided into Heavy, Medium and Light Tanks.

The heavy tank was essentially intended for attacking main trench systems. It had, therefore, to be very long to cross the wide trenches, and, consequently, heavy. The heavy tanks in the war were between 30 and 40 feet long, and weighed about 30 tons, and needed a special truck for railway transport. They were very slow, and about six miles an hour was the maximum speed that they reached, and their circuit of action seldom exceeded 40 miles, and was usually much less. Nothing more than bullet-proof armour was attempted during the war.

The Medium Tank could count on being helped across the wide trenches (by ramping the sides after

The Medium "A" Tank.

The first of the faster and lighter tanks used by the British during the Great War. Sometimes called the Whippet.

the initial attack had passed over, or by other means), and did not, therefore, need to be so long. It could, therefore, be made much lighter, and consequently faster and possessing a longer circuit of action. This was what was required for the more open warfare. It still, however, needed to be able to cross field trenches and shelled ground, and needed a fair length for this purpose. The Medium A was the first of this type, and the only one used in the war; it was the forerunner of the Vickers Medium Tank of to-day. It had a speed of about nine miles an hour on good ground, and a circuit of action of 80 miles. As a first attempt of its kind, the machine was a success, but it had certain faults. There were two engines, each driving one track, and steering was obtained by speeding up one engine or the other. This introduced many complications, *e.g.*, two gear-boxes and two sets of gears for the driver to change. These faults were put right in the next model—the Medium B—and this was replaced almost at once by a still better model —the Medium C—but neither of these models reached France in time for the war.

Light tanks were used by the French alone during the war. From the start the main idea behind the French authorities was that they could blast their way through the main trench systems with artillery and that they needed small, handy tanks that would help the infantry forward in the semi-open warfare beyond. Hence they constructed their Renault tank, which weighed only five to six tons, and could be transported up to the battlefield on a lorry, thus saving much wear and tear on the tracks. This tank could only cross quite small trenches, about three to four feet wide, and had a speed of five to six miles an hour. Our view was that the trench-crossing capacity of this tank was too small even for the semi-open warfare beyond the main trench systems, and our medium tanks could all cross a six feet gap. The French also built a few heavier tanks, and used them on occasions, but it was the Renault Tank on which they concentrated, and it assisted them very largely to gain their great victory at Soissons, in July, 1918. In this battle conditions of mobile warfare existed, and there were few trenches of any size. The conditions were, therefore, ideal for these small, handy and inconspicuous tanks.

At this time the Ministry of Munitions were working full speed on the Mark V Tank, which we hoped would begin to arrive in France early in 1918. It was practically the model that we had been offered after the Somme offensive in 1916, and which we had lost owing to delay in making a decision. This delay had cost us dearly. However, new improvements had now been incorporated, and the Mark V Tank—though it arrived late in the war—turned out to be the best heavy tank that we produced. The previous tanks had all been equipped with a Daimler sleeve-valve engine, and although this had proved to be particularly satisfactory in its working, it was underpowered for heavy tanks proof against armour-piercing bullets.

Lt.-Colonel Stern had foreseen this, and had put in hand the experimental work for a Ricardo engine with 150 horse-power. This had, fortunately, been done at an early stage, without waiting for any military demands, and it now proved to be just what was required for the Mark V Tank. This tank was the same length as the Mark I to IV tanks, and as the trench-crossing at Cambrai with fascines had caused considerable labour and difficulties, we now asked that some of the heavy tanks should be made six feet longer. We felt that this would be an insurance against the enemy digging wider trenches, in addition to making more certain of being able to cross the existing main trench systems. This was met by taking some of the Mark V tanks and adding six feet in the centre during construction. This produced what was known as the Mark V* tank, and a large number of these arrived in France towards the end of the war. They proved, however, to be under-engined and difficult to steer, owing to the great length of track on the ground, and a Mark V** tank was produced. This had a 225 h.p. Ricardo engine, and was an excellent heavy tank for assaulting main trench systems; none of these, however, reached France before the end of the war.

There was a proposal which must be related, as it had a special connection with tanks, and which occurred just before the Third Battle of Ypres. Part of the plan of this battle was that if the advance progressed according to plan it was intended to effect a landing on the Belgian Coast behind the enemy. One of the main difficulties was that along this part of the coast the sea wall was steep and had a projecting cornice at the top. In addition, there was likely to be a collection of seaweed near the bottom, which would render it very slippery. The plan was to land the 1st Division on this coast from some special large pontoons. Three tanks were to be loaded at the head of each pontoon, and they were to be the first to climb the sea wall. They were required to assist tactically in the very likely event of the landing being opposed, and they were also provided with winding gear to haul vehicles and munitions up over the sea wall. The main problem, from our point of view, was how to enable the tanks to surmount the wall, which was extremely steep near the top and sloped away below towards the sea. Here was the case of a known obstacle, and we felt as confident of crossing it as we did later over the wide trenches at Cambrai.

A model of the sea wall was made near our Headquarters at Bermicourt, and experiments started. In a short time special timber cribs had been constructed and arrangements made to carry these in front of the tank and drop them on the sea wall to form a ramp leading up and over the wall. In addition, special spuds were fitted to the tracks to cut through seaweed and obtain a grip on the concrete. These devices worked perfectly, and although the operation never took place, owing to the failure of the attack on the main front, it is reasonably certain that the tanks could have played their part successfully.

CHAPTER III.

TANKS IN 1918.

At Cambrai the Tank Corps consisted of the 1st, 2nd and 3rd Brigades, commanded respectively by Brigadier-Generals C. D'A. B. S. Baker-Carr, A. Courage and I. Hardness-Lloyd. Each brigade had three battalions, making nine battalions in all. Various proposals had been put forward for the expansion of the Tank Corps to 18 battalions, and had provisionally been approved, but shortage of infantry reinforcements caused a temporary suspension of the proposals.

The winter 1917-18 was spent in training, and great progress was made by the units in the mechanical maintenance of their tanks, which will be described later. Early in 1918 it became clear that the Germans would launch an offensive against the Allied front in the spring, and plans were made for the use of tanks to oppose them. The policy that was adopted was undoubtedly right. The tanks were distributed by battalions along a wide front where the attack was expected, and the intention was that these tanks should co-operate with infantry reserves for definite counter-attacks in the event of the enemy capturing a position within our main battle zone. By this time the Tank Corps had been increased to five brigades and 13 battalions in all. The German attack, however, met with considerable and rapid success, and much confusion resulted. In many places the main position was overrun and the infantry reserves were used as stop gaps, and the pre-arranged plans for tanks and fresh reserves being used for counter-attack could not materialise. The battle moved rapidly, and the heavy tanks, with which nearly all units were equipped, had not the mobility to keep pace. In several cases they rendered valuable assistance, but many tanks were captured through lack of petrol, or had to be destroyed to save them falling into the enemy's hands intact. As the tanks became expended, some tank units were made into Lewis gun battalions, and did valuable work. As the battle stabilised, attempts were made to reorganise the Corps, but this was hindered by the re-opening of the German offensive on the Lys. We were also threatened with large reductions in the Corps to provide reinforcements for the infantry. On April 24th the Germans attacked at Villers Bretonneux and the first tank versus tank action took place.

A German tank appeared and knocked out two of our tanks, which were armed with machine-guns only. One of our tanks armed with 6 pr. guns then appeared and knocked out the German tank, only to be knocked out itself later by an enemy field gun. Some more German tanks then appeared, but more British tanks were coming up, and the German tanks withdrew, abandoning one machine, which they left within our lines. A few other occasions occurred when the Germans made use of tanks, but as they never possessed more than 15 of their own tanks and a small number of captured tanks, these efforts were insignificant.

About the same time, and a little south of Villers Bretonneux, the first important action by our Medium Tanks took place.

Seven of our Medium A Tanks were sent up to assist in restoring the situation, and they suddenly came on to two German battalions preparing to attack. Our tanks attacked them at once, and catching them in close formation, they killed and wounded over 400 men. This was a great example of the power of fast tanks if they can catch the enemy in close formation in the open.

The German attacks now died down, and the Tank Corps settled down to a very busy period of re-arming and preparing for new battles. The Mark V Tank, which has already been described, was now arriving in considerable numbers, and these, with a smaller number of Medium A Tanks, formed the main equipment of the Tank Corps.

On August 1st the Tank Directorate in England was abolished, and Col. Fuller was sent to the War Office to inaugurate a new branch, known as S.D.7, to deal with the administration of tanks and the 1919 programme in particular. His place as G.S.O.I., Tank Corps, in France being taken by Col. H. Karslake. The old Tank Committee was abolished, being replaced by a more representative body, known as the Tank Board. The expansion of the Tank Corps had again been discussed, and the formation of a total of 34 battalions was now approved.

Before the end of June the Tank Corps were again in a position to attack, being equipped with the much-improved Mark V Tanks. The 5th Tank Brigade attacked with the Australians at Hamel. All preparations had been carefully worked out, and the infantry and tanks had trained together. The battle was an overwhelming success, and the Mark V Tanks came fully up to expectations. This was followed by an equally great success when the 9th Tank Battalion co-operated with an attack by the French at Moreuil.

These successes, and the great French victory at the battle of Soissons, which has already been referred to, paved the way for the resumption of a general offensive. On August the 8th the battle of Amiens was launched, on a three-corps front. A total of nine Heavy Tank battalions were used in the assault, leaving four battalions behind, who were re-fitting with Mark V Tanks. In addition, the 3rd Tank Brigade had two battalions of Medium A tanks, which were for use with the Cavalry Corps to exploit success. The attack resembled the battle of Cambrai in tactics, and proved a great success. A penetration was effected on the first day to a depth of $7\frac{1}{2}$ miles. The battle was continued in the succeeding days, but the lack of fresh reserves of tanks was very much felt. The Medium A Tanks, or Whippets, as they were called, had less success with cavalry. This was partly due to lack of previous training together, but it became quite clear that the close tactical co-operation of cavalry when mounted and Medium Tanks was not possible. When the going was bad the tanks were left behind; then when the cavalry were held up by machine-guns, the tanks forged ahead. But as soon as the tanks approached, the machine-guns remained silent and concealed among trees or ruins, and tanks were unable by themselves to locate and destroy the enemy machine-guns. If men work forward on foot under cover of the tanks, they can ferret out the machine-guns that would otherwise destroy them, but mounted men cannot work forward in this way against concealed machine-guns, because they cannot lie down at intervals like infantry and become inconspicuous. Previous training might have evolved a scheme whereby a small number of dismounted cavalrymen advanced, very lightly equipped, behind the tanks to mop up machine-guns and so open the way for the cavalry. The question of cavalry and tanks will be considered again later in the book when dealing with the employment of modern fighting machines.

The final result of this battle was that the enemy lost 22,000 prisoners and 400 guns. Against this, almost half the tanks had been hit by shell-fire and destroyed, or had to be evacuated for heavy repairs. This was due to the fact that the enemy had at last realised the importance of tanks. He would probably not have been able to compete with us in tank construction, due to his more limited resources, but he never intended to do so, because he did not realise their importance until too late.

The courses open to him were minefields and anti-tank guns. The former he used on occasions, but not on a large scale, and they only caused us few casualties. As regards anti-tank guns, he took no steps to start with, other than the production of a heavy anti-tank rifle, which proved quite useless; but towards the end of the war he was engaged in a large production programme of heavy anti-tank machine-guns. Until these arrived his only course was to use field guns for anti-tank work. This he did, and used as much as 30 per cent. of his field artillery at times for anti-tank work. Some of these were mobile guns, but many were dug in on the forward area and reserved for use against tanks at short range. This greatly handicapped the enemy in the proper use of his field artillery, but it was the cause of very heavy tank casualties in the battle of Amiens, and later battles.

From July, 1918, onwards, the German Command realised their great mistake. In this month Ludendorff wrote: " . . . It is to the tanks that the enemy owes his success," and an order issued by the German 51st Corps read: " . . . As soon as the tanks are destroyed the whole attack fails." In some German orders it was laid down that the main *rôle* of the artillery was anti-tank defence. Our successes were always attributed to the use of mass tank attacks, and towards the end the appearance of tanks often caused the enemy to surrender.

After the battle of Amiens the Tank Corps took part in the battle of Bapaume, the Second Battle of Arras, Epehy and Cambrai St. Quentin, and finally, the battles of the Selle and Maubeuge.

These battles followed much the same course as the Battle of Amiens, and the main lessons may be summed up as follows :—

On every occasion when tanks were used as a surprise in a properly co-ordinated plan with infantry, and protected by an artillery barrage with a proportion of smoke, the attack was an overwhelming success. The surprise lay not so much in the method of attack as in the fact that the enemy could never tell when or where the assault would take place. In every case the utmost simplicity was aimed at, and this included preliminary training between infantry and tanks, whenever possible, so that everyone knew exactly what he was required to do. These were the keynotes of our success—simplicity and surprise. On occasions we attacked without suitable artillery support, or without a well co-ordinated plan, and these were almost invariably failures. On other occasions, tanks attacked a defensive position alone or a long way ahead of the infantry, and their effect was very small. It was a suitable combination of the three arms—infantry, artillery and tanks that led to the successes in our assaults on the enemy positions.

During this period of fighting, from August 8th to the Armistice, nearly 2,000 tanks had been in action, and over 800 had been handed over to Salvage Companies for repairs, due mainly to enemy artillery fire. Large number of these were, of course, repaired at our heavy workshops.

Casualties to personnel had been heavy—nearly 600 officers and 3,000 other ranks were among the killed, wounded or missing. These casualties were, however, very small compared to the great saving which the tanks must have effected in infantry casualties, and in his final despatch Sir Douglas Haig gave full credit to the tanks, as follows:—" Since the opening of our offensive, on August 8th, tanks have been employed on every battlefield, and the importance of the part played by them in breaking up the resistance of the German infantry can scarcely be exaggerated. . . . It is no disparagement of the courage of our infantry, or the skill and devotion of our artillery to say that the achievements of these essential arms would have fallen short of the full measure of success achieved by our armies had it not been for the very gallant and devoted work of the Tank Corps, under the command of Major-General H. J. Elles."

Although these first three chapters have merely contained an outline of the war work, they cannot be closed without a brief reference to the Tank Training Centre at Home and the work of the R.A.F. with tanks and the armoured cars in France.

When we lost Col. Swinton, the Tank Training Centre at Home, which was then established at Wool, in Dorset, was taken over by General Anley, and later by Brigadier-General W. Glasgow. Owing to the rapid expansion of the Corps, and at times the heavy casualty lists, the work at this centre was very heavy, but the utmost zeal and enthusiasm prevailed. In all, they formed 41 new Tank units, which were sent out, in due course, to France.

Our co-operation during the war with the Air Force was of interest. In July, 1918, a squadron commanded by Major T. Leigh Mallory, D.S.O., was attached to the Tank Corps for co-operating with us, and for experimental work. Much of the work in battle was of a type which is now normally carried out by Army Co-operation Squadrons, but much experimental work was done in the direction of visual signalling by discs and wireless. The most important work, however, was the protection of tanks from anti-tank weapons. This was particularly successful in the Battle of Bapaume, in which a large number of enemy anti-tank guns were spotted, and shot up or bombed by the squadron before they could harm our tanks. This became an important feature in all our future battles.

Our Armoured Cars during these battles belonged to the 17th Tank Battalion, which landed in France under the command of Lt.-Col. E. J. Carter, with 16 armoured cars at the end of April, 1918. They were first attached to the 6th French Cavalry Division, which was following the retreating enemy to the River Ourcq, north of Chateau Thierry.

They were able to proceed ahead of the cavalry and open fire on enemy machine-gunners, and gave considerable assistance to the French.

Later, the battalion was withdrawn and ordered to take part in our attack in the Battle of Amiens, on August 8th. After the initial assault had taken place, the armoured cars advanced through the captured position, being helped over obstacles by tanks specially detailed for the purpose. Beyond this the roads were clear, and the cars advanced into the enemy territory. Here they had a field day. They scattered and shot down columns of transport and troops, surprised men at their meals, and effected heavy casualties in many ways.

A little later this battalion was used again in a similar manner on the First Army front, and re-repeated their successes, and they continued to operate on various fronts in this way up to the Armistice, and finally led the troops into Cologne, on December 6th.

The remarkable success of this battalion was, no doubt, partly due to the novelty and surprise of this form of attack. They had many cars hit by shell fire, but their casualties in personnel only numbered five.

It is doubtful if armoured cars to-day could produce the same results. Modern armies practice blocking the roads with guns and obstacles to stop these vehicles, and they would not have the free run that the 17th Battalion encountered. Still, it is well to remember the striking success of this small number of fighting vehicles when let loose behind the enemy front.

Lack of space prevents the inclusion of anything but a very brief reference to the work of the tanks of other nations, but this chapter cannot be closed without reference to the work of American tanks.

Mechanical warfare had a natural attraction for this great nation, and they sent officers to our headquarters to enquire into their use at the earliest possible moment. In 1917 an American Tank Corps, consisting of 25 battalions, was approved, and a huge constructional programme for tanks was initiated in America. The mass production of a machine of this nature, however, takes time, and the Americans had to start by training at British and French schools and equipping themselves with their tanks until the American machines should materialise. Units trained and equipped in this way took part in battles with British and French, as well as with American divisions, and met with striking success, in most cases. In particular, the 301st American Tank Battalion trained with the British, and worked alongside us, and showed the highest fighting qualities. The American Tank Corps would have been an even greater threat to the enemy in 1919, by which time their full power would have been developed.

CHAPTER IV.

TANK CHARACTERISTICS AND EXPERIMENTS DURING THE WAR.

THE general characteristics of the fighting tanks were described in the first chapters, in order to show the way in which the mechanical and tactical developments progressed side by side; but there are many interesting and important points which could not be dwelt on in these chapters without confusing the story.

A point of special interest was the fact that the first five Marks of Heavy Tank were exactly identical in outline, shape and size. At the time when the first tanks were being designed, trench warfare had already set in, and although the terrible condition that the ground would reach in future battles was not foreseen, it was realised that there would be shell holes and craters to cross as well as trenches. The above-mentioned shape, with its up-turned prow, enabled tanks to nose their way in and out of obstacles which could not have been otherwise negotiated, and so successful did it prove that the shape was retained throughout the war for the heavy tanks. It had, however, one objection; with an all-round track of this nature the armament had either to fire from between the front horns which then acted as blinkers and restricted the view, or through the tracks from sponsons on

THE ALLIED TANK.

The Allied Tank, which was called the Mark VIII by the British and the Liberty Tank by the Americans. It would have been made in very large numbers if the war had continued in 1919.

either side. The disadvantage of these sponsons has already been referred to, namely, the fact that they had to contain either a machine gun or a 6-pr. gun but could not contain both.

Towards the end of the war, however, an allied conference was held to discuss tank design, and a tank known as the Mark VIII was designed which was to be produced in very large numbers for our offensive in 1919 if this had become necessary. This tank was some 6 ft. longer than the Marks I to V, but was otherwise similar in general appearance and characteristics. With the greater length it was found possible to arrange for both a 6-pr. gun and a machine gun to fire from each side of the tank with a suitable arc of fire. It was estimated that a total of 6,000 of these tanks would be constructed for 1919; the Liberty Engine from America was to be used, the armour and transmission were to come mostly from England, and a huge factory for the erection of these tanks was constructed near Paris. Actually, very few of these tanks were built as the Armistice intervened, but they would have been an excellent type of heavy tank for breaking through a main trench system.

The reader has now been introduced to Marks I to V, Mark V*, and Mark V** and Mark VIII, and may be wondering what happened to the intermediate Marks.

The Mark VI was an experimental model with hydraulic transmission using a Williams-Janney variable speed gear, and had a new type of fighting body with one 6-pr. gun only. A few of these machines, but with the same fighting body as the Mark IV, were made and known as the Mark VII. Some experimental machines were also made using petrol-electric transmission.

A tank fitted with either of these forms of transmission is delightful to drive; the tank can be controlled without physical effort, and all the troubles, such as the periodical tightening of epicyclic brake bands, etc., are forgotten; but the electrical transmission is complicated and not likely to be really reliable for this type of work until considerable progress in detail design has been made. Both types had the disadvantage that it would have been very difficult to arrange for the bulk supply of the rather tricky transmission apparatus, and they were abandoned in favour of the improved epicyclic transmission designed by Major Wilson.

When we came to the design of Medium tanks we had more latitude as regards shape and size. These tanks were definitely not required to fight among the craters and main trench systems. It was, therefore, possible to use lower tracks and shoot over the top of them; this method was adopted and enabled us to have a gun and machine-gun in each tank, and the design eventually led to the central revolving turret of the Medium tank of to-day. We did not, however, reach this stage during the war.

The only real necessity for a gun on a tank is to enable it to take on enemy tanks or knock out an anti-tank weapon which is protected by armour.

The Medium "C" Tank.

A very successful tank which appeared just after the Armistice, and formed the main equipment of the post-war Tank Corps.

For all other purposes a machine-gun is far more suitable, and as there was little indication of the appearance of enemy tanks, all the earlier Medium tanks were armed with machine-guns only. The Medium A has already been described in Chapter II. The Medium B followed, but only small numbers were made owing to the introduction of the Medium C. The early models of the Medium C were equipped with machine guns only and they formed the main equipment of the post-war Tank Corps, but before the end of the war a Medium C Tank was designed with one 6-pr. gun and two machine-guns; if the war had continued large numbers of this type would have been made and they would have provided us with an excellent medium tank for semi-open warfare, equally capable of assisting our troops with machine-gun fire or attacking enemy tanks with the gun.

There was one Mark of tank known as Mark IX which should be mentioned. At one time it was considered that if we could carry up behind armour protection a large number of machine-gun detachments, take them through the enemy and deposit them on a final objective, it would provide a cheap way of winning the war. It is doubtful if the policy was sound except in certain special cases, but about 35 Mark IX tanks were made for this purpose. They were heavy tanks, about 32 ft. long, and had a clear carrying space in the centre which could just hold 50 men or 10 tons of stores. The armament had to be limited to two automatic rifles in front when carrying full load. When the carrying space was not fully occupied additional automatic rifles could be fired from the sides of the machine. The tank was not very successful mechanically, being under-engined, and the occupants suffered considerable discomfort from heat and fumes; and after a few attempts to use these machines the idea was abandoned.

Signal tanks were used during the war with a little success on occasions. They were Mark IV Tanks with the armament removed from the sponsons and wireless apparatus carried instead in a sound-proof room. Wireless was not, however, sufficiently advanced in those days to give real value in this way.

The gun-carrying tank was another type that was constructed and tried during the war. Mechanically it was on the lines of the Mark IV Tank, but with a lower track. It could carry either a 4.5-in. or 6-in. howitzer or 60-pr. gun on a platform between the front horns of the machine. There was a small cab on either side which gave flank protection and accommodated two drivers, and the gun shield itself gave some frontal protection. The gun could be fired from the machine or removed in a few minutes and used on the ground. This tank carried a considerable quantity of gun ammunition, and it was for this purpose that it was chiefly used. The question of the haulage of guns and the supply of ammunition was dealt with in other ways later, which will be described in other chapters, but this first type of gun carrier, though it gave us ideas and practical experience, was not on the right lines mechanically, and only a few were made and used during the war.

These trials with Signal Tanks and Gun Carriers made us realise that we would need an experimental establishment in France. How wide a trench could the tanks cross and how could we assist them over wider ones? How could you stop the molten lead from bullets entering the crevices round turrets? These, and many other problems were constantly arising; there was not time to refer such matters to the Minister of Munitions at home, nor were they sufficiently in the picture to understand our real difficulties in these ways. A small experimental establishment was, therefore, initiated; it was controlled mainly by Lt.-Col. P. Johnson, who carried out some remarkable work.

The crossing of wide trenches by the use of fascines has already been described, and these fascines were later replaced by a hexagonal crib work of timber and steel. This was far handier and lighter an article and could be unbolted and packed up into a small space. Large numbers of these were made and kept in store ready for use if required.

The question of "splash" was one which caused us much trouble and necessitated experimental work. When a bullet hits a steel plate, the heat generated fuses the lead and this squirts along the armour plate and enters the tank at any crevices that exist, such as the clearance between a revolving turret and the walls of the tank. This lead enters the tank as a bright flash, and is known as splash.

If it strikes the skin little particles of lead penetrate and cause loss of blood but not a serious wound; these flashes, however, often caused blindness when they struck the eye during the war. If several enemy machine guns were playing on a tank the splash was often very serious and sometimes the whole crew would be rendered out of action for the time being. Trials were made with fireproof felt packing round crevices and a good deal was done to reduce the danger. The crews wore goggles with triplex glass and chain masks over their faces which gave them considerable protection.

It is curious that the Germans never realised the effect of splash on our crews; they fired armour-piercing bullets which had little effect, but in no orders or instructions did they ever refer to the undoubted value of machine-gun fire with normal ammunition for producing splash.

Many of our tank crews were convinced that the trouble was largely due to the flaking of small pieces of steel from the plates on the inside of the tanks, but though this no doubt happened at times, our trials at our experimental establishment proved that the main cause of these minor wounds was the entering of molten lead through crevices.

All new types of tank had to pass as being fighting fit on their first arrival from home. The test for splash consisted of sitting in the bottom of the tank and watching for the tell-tale flashes while a machine-gun fired at the tank. The tanks varied considerably; in one tank the turrets had been so badly fitted that a bullet entered almost intact and wounded an officer who was sitting observing inside the tank and the red flag had to be hoisted, which was the signal to the machine-gunner to stop firing. The tanks were then handed over to the workshops for adjustment of turrets, fitting felt pads and many other detail alterations which we found necessary. Reports were also sent home to the Ministry of Munitions so that future batches of tanks could be fitted in this way before being sent out, but it was always necessary to make many minor additions and alterations to tanks in France. It would have had a disturbing effect on the mass-production programmes at home if we had asked for constant minor changes, and we adopted the policy of carrying these out ourselves in France and having them incorporated in the next production series at home.

The question of removing barbed wire obstacles by means of tanks was another question which was investigated by our experimental branch. The path left by a tank after passing through a wire entanglement was quite passable to infantry and required no improvement; the only point to watch was that a second tank should not attempt to make a second path less than 30 yards to a flank; if it did so the effect of pressing down the wires in this second path often caused sufficient tension in them to raise the wires in the first path and so make it difficult for the infantry to cross. These paths were, however, unsuitable for the passage of a large number of cavalry and new methods had to be devised, and, after a few trials, a method was produced which proved surprisingly successful. Three tanks were used, each towing a large heavy grapnel by means of a 3-inch steel wire rope. The first tank passed right through the obstacle, the grapnel catching and breaking all the longitudinal strands in the entanglement, so that a narrow clean cut was made right through the obstacle. The other two tanks now advanced and crossed the obstacle a few yards on either side of this cut. The grapnels gathered up the strands of wire, and just as they reached the far edge of the entanglement the tanks turned outwards and moved parallel to the wire and a few yards away from it. The grapnel behind each of these two tanks now contained all the longitudinal strands which were caught up among the barbs, and as the grapnel was dragged in the new direction along the wire these strands rolled over and over like a great cable and every single picket or strand of wire was swept up by this kind of snowball which collected round the grapnel. A hundred yards of the heaviest wire entanglements could be cleared in this way quite easily and in a few minutes, leaving absolutely no trace of wire on the ground. The operation could, of course, be carried out more slowly with two or even one tank if necessary. Large gaps of this nature were made in the wire at the Cambrai battle, after the infantry assault had passed over, to enable the cavalry to advance without delay. Later

TANK CHARACTERISTICS AND EXPERIMENTS.

on a proposal was made that a few tanks should pass over on moonlight nights and steal large stretches of wire which the Germans had so laboriously constructed on their whole front, but this was vetoed as being a side issue. It could have been carried out quite easily during the winter months, but tanks were scarce and units wanted all the time they could obtain during the winter for training.

The unditching beam was an early device which was produced to enable our tanks to extricate themselves during the period that they were being used on shell-torn ground; it was retained for use throughout the war with heavy tanks, though there was less necessity for it in the later stages of the war. It consisted of a heavy iron-shod timber beam about two foot longer than the width of the tank. This beam was normally carried across and on top of the tank and could be fastened by short chains to the tracks. At a later date arrangements were made so that this process of fastening the beam to the tracks could be carried out by putting out a hand from a cab on the top of the tank and without exposing any men to fire. Special rails were provided to enable the beam to follow round over the top of the tank with the tracks and clear any cabs or turrets. Now the usual cause of a tank becoming held up by the ground was the sinking of the tracks until the weight was taken by the belly of the tank and the tracks then revolved uselessly. Sometimes the belly of the tank would be caught on a tree trunk or a concealed lump of masonry from a destroyed building, and the effect was the same. When this occurred the beam was fastened to the tracks and as it passed under the tracks it cleared away the obstacle or lifted the tank bodily off it. The beam could also be used to enable the tank to climb a very steep but short slope, such as might be met on a railway embankment or in emerging from a wide trench into which the tail of the tank had dropped. The tank was, of course, unable to steer while the beam was in use. Many tanks succeeded in extricating themselves from difficulties in this way during the war and were thus enabled to continue to play their allotted part in the battle instead of having to wait until they were pulled out.

The production of smoke clouds for screening the tanks was another direction in which much work was carried out. Two methods were tried experimentally, and they were the same in principle as two out of the three methods which are being tried to-day. The first was the insertion of sulphonic acid into the exhaust pipe of the tank, causing heavy smoke clouds to be emitted from the exhaust. The second was the mounting of a 6-inch Newton Mortar between the rear horns of a tank; this could fire either high explosive or smoke bombs. Both methods were demonstrated on several occasions and the latter appeared particularly promising, but shortage of tanks, lack of time for training and the difficulties under stress of war prevented any actual trial in battle.

Many other minor experiments and trials were made, such as the use of mechanical semaphore arms and coloured lights for signalling, sound trumpets for listening for tanks, nets for camouflage and other devices for concealing tanks, but these would not be of special interest to-day. The signalling apparatus for use between tanks proved too complicated for hasty wartime training, and we used coloured flags in much the same manner as the Tank Corps uses them to-day.

Considerable work was carried out in connection with the passage of tanks over obstacles and over the question of supplies for tanks in battle. The former is dealt with in Chapter XII, in which the whole subject is reviewed up to the present time. The latter is dealt with in the next chapter.

CHAPTER V.

THE TANK AS A TRANSPORT VEHICLE.

ONE of the main lessons from the Great War is the difficulty of the Administrative side in arranging for the necessary supplies of food, ammunition and petrol to maintain the fighting troops and to enable them to retain their mobility during offensive operations against the enemy. This was naturally very marked on the Western Front; under the trench warfare conditions both sides maintained large armies along the front by the assistance of a network of railways, light railways and roads, and transportation was taxed to a maximum to compete with requirements. When an offensive was launched the troops advanced over an area in which all these means of transportation had been destroyed by shell fire if not by enemy demolitions, and our transport facilities were often reduced to limbered wagons and pack animals. It was quite impossible for such methods to compete with our requirements, and this was one of the main causes of delay and eventual stabilisation in nearly every offensive in France; this question was causing our army grave concern in our final offensive before the Armistice. This difficulty had been foreseen at an early stage by the Tank Corps, and some of the out-of-date tanks were turned into supply tanks as new models arrived. To start with,

THE TANK AS A TRANSPORT VEHICLE. 53

each battalion was given six supply tanks—*i.e.*, two per company; these tanks were stripped of armament and all unnecessary weight and could carry five tons of stores each.

They were used to a small extent at the Third Battle of Ypres, and to a much greater extent later when the tanks were operating on more suitable ground.

In 1918 the supply tanks were formed into companies—one with each Brigade and with a strength of six tanks for each battalion in that brigade. These companies did splendid work on many occasions. In addition to supplying petrol, oil and ammunition for tanks, they often assisted by carrying up large quantities of ammunition and **R.E.** material for other troops, which would otherwise have needed prohibitive numbers of men or pack animals to carry these quantities over the ground in the forward areas.

In addition to supply tanks we produced sledges for trailing behind tanks. The advantage of this system was that stores could be taken up by fighting tanks which were moving up in reserve, and dumped on the sledges in the forward area when the tank went into action. In addition, the stores needed no unpacking such as was necessary with the supply tanks, and provided a neat ready-made dump when the sledges were unhooked at their destination. Three sledges, carrying a total of ten tons of stores, could be towed behind tanks of the Mark V type.

Such was the success of this work carried out by

our supply tanks that considerable interest was aroused, and as a result it was eventually decided to order 10,000 tractors from America for the purpose of hauling up supplies to the forward areas for our proposed offensive in 1919. The Armistice, however, arrived before any of these tractors had been delivered, except for a few experimental models.

The value of this type of cross-country traction was not limited to the fact, that it was the only type of transport that could come anywhere near filling the required demands; there were important economic aspects also. One of the greatest difficulties during the war was the overseas transport of food and fodder in the face of the enemy submarine campaign, and any material reduction in requirements that could be effected was of the greatest assistance. Tractors, and especially somewhat crude machines of the tank or Holt tractor type, are inefficient machines economically compared to lorries on roads, but even then they showed large economic savings compared with the fodder requirements of the limbered wagons or pack animals which would be needed to carry out the same work. In fact, figures were prepared by Major S. H. Foot, D.S.O., R.E., who initiated this train of thought; he estimated that there were about half a million horses in France used for transport and artillery traction, and that these consumed some 80,000 tons of fodder per month. If it had been possible to change this horse transport into suitable tractors the consumption in petrol and oil would have been about 40,000 tons* in weight and a great deal smaller in bulk, which is important from a shipping point of view. But this is on the supposition that the tractors were in continued use; horses eat the same ration while at work or at rest, whereas tractors consume nothing while at rest. Hence the actual saving to our overseas shipping would probably have been in the neighbourhood of at least 60,000 tons a month. In addition the saving in personnel would have been in the neighbourhood of 50 per cent.* also. A further point was the security against night bombing by enemy aeroplanes. Transport lines were suffering very heavy casualties from night bombing and little could be done to avoid this, whereas the tractors that might have taken their place could have been scattered or run into little hollows or trenches, and would have in any case been far less vulnerable. There was thus an overwhelming case for the introduction of cross-country tractors or lorries during the war if the right vehicles could be produced, and this led to the order which has already been mentioned for large deliveries of tractors from America.

In fact in all its work the tank was really used as a transport vehicle carrying forward machine-guns and ammunition and men, and it was, therefore, as a transport vehicle that it effected such

---

* Tractors would have needed spare parts and personnel for manufacture and repair, which would have been in excess of any similar remount or veterinary requirement for horses, and these figures allow for this.

great savings in lives and time on the battlefield. This realisation led Colonel Fuller to produce a paper called Tank Economics at Headquarters Tank Corps in July, 1918. It was a remarkable paper and the following is a summary of some of the more important points.

Man-Power.

Owing to the fact that the tank provides a form of transport using mechanical power, the number of men required to keep a gun in action is greatly reduced compared with the other arms.

An Artillery Brigade requires 32.6 men per gun.

A Machine Gun Battalion requires 14.5 men per gun.

A Wing R.A.F. (4 Squadrons) requires 5.9 men per gun.

A Tank Battalion requires 3.1 men per gun.

Casualties.

Great reductions in casualties were effected by the use of tanks, and corresponding increase in the proportion of enemy casualties.

During the preliminary bombardment at the Third Battle of Ypres we suffered 10,000 casualties from enemy counter-bombardment. At Cambrai tanks were substituted for this bombardment and preliminary casualties were practically nil.

On the first day of the assault at the Battle of the Somme, casualties amounted to 40,000. In the

THE TANK AS A TRANSPORT VEHICLE. 57

case of the Third Battle of Ypres they were 16,000 and in both cases the enemy casualties were considerably smaller than ours. In the Battle of Cambrai on the first day our casualties numbered 4,000, and we captured 8,000 prisoners.

Shells.

In the Third Battle of Ypres the preliminary bombardment on a 17,000 yard front used 93,000 tons of shells and the cost of manufacturing and firing these shells was approximately £465,000. At the Battle of Cambrai there was no preliminary bombardment and only 5,000 tons of shells were fired on the first day. The 400 tanks used at this battle cost about £2,000,000, whereas the shells employed during the Battle of Arras cost £10,000,000, and the shells had no residual value, whereas tanks usually lasted for two or three battles. Over 17,000 tanks could have been built for the cost of the preliminary bombardment at the Third Battle of Ypres.

Time.

In all economics the most important factor is the economy of time. The tank was pre-eminently a time-saving machine in France.

At Cambrai a penetration of 10,000 yards was effected from a base of 13,000 yards in 12 hours. At Ypres from a base of 17,000 yards a similar depth of penetration took three months.

CHAPTER VI.

TANK MECHANICAL ENGINEERING.

As the Tank Corps was the first fighting formation to employ mechanical means of transport in battle, we had to evolve our own ideas about the mechanical maintenance of these machines. It was, of course, a matter of the first importance, and just as horsemanship is of primary importance to cavalry, so the art of keeping the machines in first-class mechanical condition became one of the first duties of a Tank Corps Unit. This was not, however, the case from the start. When the first units were formed there was little time to train tank drivers, and R.A.S.C. drivers were employed to drive the tank, and the R.A.S.C. officers naturally initiated the system of workshops and repairs for the first Tank units, on the lines of R.A.S.C. units. This, however, was unsound in principle; R.A.S.C. units in the early part of the Great War had perforce to employ many different types of civilian lorries and they were even mixed in units. It was, therefore, necessary to attach small travelling workshops to these units to manufacture or alter parts for repairing the lorries. The possibility of obtaining and stocking sufficient spare parts, for such a large number of different types of vehicle, and ensuring that these were always available for units that were working near the front, was out of the question, at any rate in the early part of the war. Hence the need for these travelling workshops, and the same system was adopted by the R.A.S.C. who joined the first few Tank units.

So long as we only had a few units in the Tank Corps this system did not matter very much. The unit shops carried out experimental work and made urgent spare parts and carried out all repairs. This system was welcomed by the unit Commanders, most of whom had unfortunately no mechanical knowledge at all, and they were quite content to concentrate on the tactical side and weapon training and leave the messy mechanical side to the experts.

The two main objections to this method were as follows. Firstly, if we expanded to a large Corps—which we had every intention of doing—it would have been impossible at this stage of the war to enlist sufficient mechanics to man a workshop for every unit. Secondly, the policy of leaving all the repair and maintenance work to the workshop personnel meant that the tank crews learnt nothing about their machines. The workshops became a little band of heroes who were called on to carry out the whole of the mechanical work without assistance from the crews, and they worked all day and night.

Both sides, however, preferred this system. The mechanics preferred to work all night rather than have their machines " messed about " by the amateur Tank crews, and the Tank Corps were more interested in their weapons than the engines and transmission of the tanks. The plunge, however, had to be taken, and it was against a good deal of opposition that General Elles instituted a new system of mechanical maintenance for the Tank Corps. In this work we were greatly assisted by Colonel F. Searle, who joined us from civilian life to run the mechanical side and brought with him a wealth of experience in this type of work. The system which we introduced is worth studying as it has been largely adopted for the army to-day, though some essential features have unfortunately been omitted; this will be discussed in a later chapter.

This system was a very simple one in principle; it was based on the policy that the Tank crews were themselves responsible for the mechanical maintenance of their tanks and that no manufacture or repair of damaged parts was to be carried out in the field. Spare parts were to be available, and these were to be substituted for the damaged parts, which would then be sent back for repair at central workshops in rear. The difficulty which the R.A.S.C. had been faced with, in having to deal with large numbers of different types of lorries, was non-existent in the Tank Corps. We never had more than three types of tank in commission at the same time in the whole Corps, and the spare part problem was, therefore, comparatively easy.

The change over to the new system was made in two stages; this was done to meet the fears expressed by many unit commanders and which

TANK MECHANICAL ENGINEERING.   61

afterwards proved to be unfounded. The first stage consisted of withdrawing all Battalion Workshops and organising one Brigade Workshop for each brigade. This was done in 1917, and early in 1918 Brigade Workshops were abolished, leaving one Central Workshop at Bermicourt; this Central Workshop could, however, send out one or more advanced shops which could be set up when required in the back areas on the portion of the front on which tanks were operating. The system was then as follows. There was a Junior Workshop Officer and N.C.O. with each company, and they had a maintenance lorry, which carried hand tools and certain special maintenance tools. If any damage occurred to a tank it was inspected by the Workshop Officer and the crew were told what to do and the Workshop Officer indented for a new spare part. The replacement of this part was carried out by the crew under the supervision of the Company Workshop Officer or his N.C.O. In addition the crews kept their own tanks mechanically fit, carrying out adjustments to brake bands, etc., themselves. Here, again, they were assisted by the workshop staff with advice but not with labour. The Workshop Officer would periodically inspect the tanks and advise the Company Commander as to their mechanical fitness, and the work carried out by the crews.

To assist the Tank Crews in their work the Chief Mechanical Engineer of the Tank Corps had a pamphlet prepared showing exactly how to replace any damaged part of a tank. Some of these parts such as sprockets and tracks were very heavy in these war time tanks, and special levers and devices were needed to remove them. It was these maintenance tools that were carried in the maintenance lorry. In addition this lorry carried a jib crane which could be fastened on the nose of a tank. In this way, if a tank was broken down away from a road with, say, a badly damaged engine, a sound tank could take the crane, approach the damaged tank, lift out the engine bodily and bring it to the road and lower it into a lorry. A new engine would then be replaced in the same way and the tank could then move under its own power.

The above is a brief description of the system of mechanical maintenance in a company. At Battalion Headquarters there was a workshop officer, who was usually a captain. His duty was to supervise the work of the workshop staff with the companies and assist the Battalion Commander in his periodical mechanical inspection of the tanks in the battalion. Thus the responsibility for the mechanical fitness of the tanks was thrown directly on to the commanding officers and tank crews, the workshop staff being there merely as advisers.

In a similar way there was a more senior workshop officer at Brigade Headquarters, and the whole of the work was co-ordinated at Tank Corps H.Q. under the Chief Mechanical Engineer. In addition to the above work, all workshop officers had the very important rôle of watching the mechanical side of the tanks, reporting any weaknesses the moment they appeared and diagnosing the mechanical troubles. It may be thought that the men who were enlisted for the Tank Corps had, previously, knowledge of this type of work; this was the case when the first few units were formed, but as we expanded the men differed in no way from the infantry recruits. The crews were taught how to maintain their tanks mechanically fit, and how to replace parts in just the same way as men are taught about field guns or machine guns, and the fact that there were so few mechanical breakdowns in the tanks during the last part of the war is proof that the system was a sound one.

This system resulted in a great saving of skilled labour. By the first method, when each unit had its own workshop and carried out its own repair work, many skilled men with different trades had to be kept with each of these workshops—fitters, turners, electricians, smiths, copper-smiths, etc. Few of these men were in continuous employment at their trades, and they were often doing labourers' work on the tanks. By stopping all repair work up in the forward areas, and replacing damaged parts and bringing all these parts back to centralised shops behind the front for repair, a great saving was effected. For instance, by the first method it was necessary to have one electrician with each workshop; there was not, however, enough work in each unit to keep them fully employed at their trades. By the second method far smaller numbers were sufficient for carrying out the repair work on the electrical gear for all tanks in central shops, because they were then used for this work and nothing else.

This method, however, necessitated a very efficient and reliable plan for the supply of spare parts. Without this, the whole system would have broken down. Our first difficulty was to persuade the Ministry of Munitions at home to supply these parts. Other corps, such as the R.A.S.C., were carrying on with workshop units and were making or repairing their own spare parts to a large extent, and the Ministry wanted us to do the same. The production of a large percentage of spare parts was bound to reduce their output programme in tanks and their figures would look less spectacular. Yet it was obviously wrong that we should use valuable skilled men for making spare parts by hand with poor workshop facilities in the field, while automatic machines could be making them at home with unskilled labour. The whole question revolved on our ability to predict accurately our requirements in spare parts. It would have been easy for us in France to demand large quantities of spare parts so as to be sure that we would never be short, but this would very definitely have reduced the number of tanks which we could expect from home with no equivalent saving in France. What was required was a set of figures based on experience as to the rate of wear and tear on the various parts of the tank and this we set out to obtain.

Every tank commander had to fill up a small and simple daily log sheet showing the hours of running, the nature of the ground passed over, the consumption in petrol and oil, and any spare parts used. In addition a number of specific tests for the wear of tracks and sprockets were carried out at H.Q. Tank Corps. All these figures were tabulated by the Chief Mechanical Engineer at H.Q. Tank Corps, and as a result he worked out a table of what spares he required for a year's running with every type of tank. On this we made demands on the Ministry of Munitions; they were, however, alarmed at our figures, and were afraid of falling below the promised production figures in tanks, and to start with they failed to produce the spare parts. It then became necessary for us to threaten to refuse to accept new tanks from home and to send them back to be broken up into spare parts at home. In the end our figures were accepted, and it then became the custom when working out figures for the output of tanks to consider a tank together with the necessary spare parts for one year as one unit and not just tanks alone. This was a sound scheme and one which might be copied to-day with advantage.

The figures were interesting. First of all, the sprockets for driving the tracks wore out very rapidly, and we had to demand large numbers as spares. Then the Ministry produced a nickel chrome steel sprocket which lasted well, but the track links then wore more rapidly. We had, therefore, to be constantly adjusting our figures and informing the Ministry of Munitions accordingly. In the end we established a good liaison with them and everything worked quite smoothly.

All spare parts were sent to our central stores near Bermicourt. To these were added the parts that had been sent back from units and had been repaired in our shops. When operations were about to take place, advanced stores were sent up and opened behind that portion of the front; these advanced stores were supplied from the central stores. Unit workshop officers drew their requirements in spare parts from these stores.

So far we have dealt with the normal repair and maintenance of the tanks, but have not referred to the course of action when a tank was seriously damaged such as by shell fire. If the tank had an ordinary mechanical breakdown it was dealt with by the crew, but if the tank was seriously damaged or if the unit was withdrawn or moved to another part of the front, then the tank was handed over to a salvage unit. These were later named Tank Field Companies. They often had to deal with tanks that had been badly knocked about and had to carry out repair work on the tank before it could be moved. They were, therefore, equipped with a small mobile workshop. Sometimes they were able to repair a damaged tank quite quickly and hand it back to a unit, but the more usual course was to make it mobile and then send it back to central shops for repairs. The work of these units was particularly dangerous. They often had to work on tanks that lay in no man's land and carry out the repair work under most difficult conditions. They were a combatant branch of the Tank Corps and were justly proud of their work.

The important experimental work carried out by the workshop staff in France has already been referred to in Chapter IV. This was kept separate from the normal repair work of the central workshops and they had their own small workshops near Bermicourt. The central shops had to work under great pressure at times in preparation for battle, and often had to meet sudden demands, such as for the construction of fascines for the Cambrai battle; they were part and parcel of the tank corps, and worked with unremitting zeal throughout the war.

In view of the recent decision to introduce a fourth branch of the staff at G.H.Q. in war to represent the Master-General of the Ordnance and deal with technical questions, it is interesting to study our experience in this direction in the Tank Corps during the war. We were a completely mechanized formation and a comparison of our work with that of a G.H.Q. which has to deal with a largely mechanized force under modern conditions is not unreal. Our Chief Mechanical Engineer, Colonel Searle, was a Commander and Adviser but not a Staff Officer. Under his direct orders came the central shops and stores, which, in turn, sent out advanced shops and stores behind the front on which the tanks were operating. In addition he commanded the experimental establishment and the salvage units. He issued technical instructions to his workshop officers who were attached to brigades. As Chief Mechanical Engineer he had direct access to General Elles, and it was as a result of discussions with his Commander that the Tank Corps technical policy was formed. Although this policy would not be entirely suitable in the army of to-day, it was an ideal policy at the time and contained many points worth studying, and some of them might well be copied to-day.

CHAPTER VII.

PLANS FOR 1919.

EARLY in 1918 we began to realise at H.Q. Tank Corps that we were living from hand to mouth over tank design. It took a year from the design of a tank to the time when it appeared in production. If, therefore, we needed any new type of tank for 1919 now was the time to consider the question. As regards immediate requirements we knew that the Mark V Tank was an excellent machine and would be coming out in considerable numbers, and we knew that they were working at a Medium Tank at home that should suit our requirements for semi-mobile warfare. Was there any other type of tank that might be essential for us in 1919? A technical committee was appointed at H.Q. Tank Corps which was instructed to consider these and several other technical questions. There was a strong feeling that we should press for experimental work at home on a type of tank that was far ahead of existing types in speed and general performance. If it failed little harm would be done. If it succeeded then we would be able to spring a surprise on the enemy in 1919 with a machine for which they were unprepared. Gradually ideas began to form, and it was Col. Fuller who eventually cleared the ground with definite proposals.

We had been suffering considerable casualties to our tanks from anti-tank artillery fire, and we realised that this would increase. Actually our casualties from this cause rose as high as 50 per cent. in the tank battles towards the end of the war. As a first step, therefore, it was decided that we must do all we could to put this right. The faster and handier tanks that we were getting would help. They were also better designed from a fighting point of view. The officer was given a turret from which he could look out and command his tank, and the laryngaphone* was tried as a means of communication within the tank. Further efforts were made to reduce splash from machine-gun fire, because, although the Germans had not yet discovered the full value of splash, they might do so later, and we had instances of one or two tanks being completely dominated and put out of action by the concentrated fire of half-a-dozen machine-guns. Great attention was also paid to tank gunnery.

In all this work, however, we were up against a real difficulty. The anti-tank gunner had such a far easier task. In spite of all efforts to do so it was unusual for any tank commander to be able to spot the anti-tank gun till it had fired, and as they usually reserved their fire for close range the first shot was often fatal. Although in peace time it is possible to train tank commanders to improve con-

---

* The laryngaphone is a type of telephone in which the transmitter is held against the throat, and thus transmits no noise other than vibrations of the larynx. All other noises in the tank are excluded.

siderably in spotting likely places for anti-tank guns and concentrating the fire from the tank on them, yet in war, with the reduced visibility due to splash, and the general noise and tumult in the forefront of the battle, the difficulty from the point of view of the tank is a very real one, and one which is, perhaps, not entirely appreciated to-day.

But it was not in connection with this work that Col. Fuller pressed his new proposals. That everything should be done to produce the best possible tank force equipped with heavy and medium tanks to fight against the enemy defences was obvious, but in addition Col. Fuller proposed that if really fast tanks could be manufactured they should be used by themselves against the enemy headquarters and communications. He likened the former work to beating a man all over his body till he bled to death, whereas the latter was like pressing a pin straight into his brain. In other words, he proposed to attack the enemy's brain and arteries so that the body would move about aimlessly and then wither away.

Our outline proposals were that these fast tanks should pass right through the enemy's defensive system—possibly by night on a moonlit night. They would do this either on the front to be attacked or to a flank of this attack. At dawn they would traverse up and down well behind the enemy front, scattering headquarters, destroying aerodromes and munition dumps and cutting important communications. It was thought that telegraph and telephone wires should be left for the first few hours. This would give the enemy the chance to spread the panic and cause order and counter-order to become thoroughly epidemic. The wires would then be cut to prevent any co-ordinated plan being made for resistance against the tanks. The enemy would then be attacked frontally by normal formations assisted by large numbers of tanks, and it was thought that a combination of these two attacks, the one at his brains and arteries and the other at his body, should lead to an overwhelming victory.

It was now necessary to prepare a general specification for this tank, which became known as the Medium D, and persuade the Ministry of Munitions to carry out the experimental work. From a military point of view we wanted a tank that could cross fairly big trenches, as these protected the whole enemy front, and we wanted to be able to cross these rapidly and without a preliminary operation to make crossing places. This meant a fairly long tank, though we counted on using various devices if we had to cross one or two lines of specially wide trenches; the length of the tank was finally settled at 30 ft. over all.

The next point was the question of weight. Any tank that had so far been built and which was 30 ft. long had weighed about 30 tons. This weight would, however, have prevented the tank from crossing many existing bridges behind the enemy front. It was therefore decided that the tank must not weigh more than 20 tons.

The tank was to be capable of crossing any

PLANS FOR 1919.

natural obstacles that would be likely to be met, and the speed was to be at least 20 miles an hour on the level or up slopes of one-in-thirty on good going. It was to carry sufficient petrol and oil for a circuit of 200 miles.

The questions of armament and ammunition to be carried were left open until the preliminary experimental work had given us some results. It was realised that as these tanks would be operating well behind the front their armament would be less important than their mobility. It was thought that in order to save weight the crew would have to be kept down to two or three and that some of the tanks would have one machine-gun and others a 6-pr. gun. The armour was to be proof against armour-piercing bullets.

This, then, was the general specification which we prepared in July, 1918, for the Medium D Tank. As regards the numbers we required it was difficult to suggest figures till we knew more about the possibilities of such a tank and when it would be ready to go into production, but 300 was suggested as a suitable number for this work of attacking enemy headquarters and communications behind the front of the main attack.

Our whole programme in outline for 1919, from a Tank Corps point of view was therefore as follows. An attack on the enemy main defences frontally, and for this purpose 3,000 tanks were being ordered. These tanks were to be mainly Mark VIII and Medium C Tanks in about equal numbers. This attack by all arms would be maintained and prevented from petering out through lack of munitions and food by the 10,000 tractors which were on order from America. Simultaneous with this attack would be the attack by the Medium D Tanks acting alone against the enemy headquarters and communications. We were thus guiding Tank Corps policy as early as in 1918, in the direction of a division, between the tanks to carry out the work of the mobile troops and those required for the close fighting. This division in war between the mobile troops and the combat troops has existed from the earliest days, though the importance of the one has at times been so great that the other has almost ceased to exist. The particular operations that we were considering for 1919 were, of course, a special case due to the existence of a strong defensive position along the whole front, but the policy of fast tanks for the long distance work, delaying all movements in the rear areas and generally paralysing the work of the enemy behind the front, and of slower, harder hitting tanks for the main battle was a sound and simple one. We will see later that this policy lapsed soon after the war, causing much confusion of thought, but has now been to some extent revived in our latest thoughts about armoured formations.

We realized that our general specification for the Medium D Tank was a very long way ahead of anything that had been made, and that it might be impossible to manufacture, but we pressed for experimental trials. As a further point we realized that the progress of these tanks behind the enemy lines might be limited by water obstacles, and that the enemy might have strong anti-tank defences at the only existing bridges. We therefore asked that the question of the floating capability of the tank should be considered with a view to its floating across water obstacles, propelling itself across with its tracks. The whole problem was a very difficult one mechanically, but it was tackled in an undaunted manner by Lt.-Col. P. Johnson, who was then on the Staff of the Chief Mechanical Engineer at H.Q. Tank Corps.

One of the most important points was to cut down all unnecessary weight, and yet it was obvious that a high speed tank of this nature would need a sprung track which at first sight appeared to mean a considerable increase in weight. After considerable study of the problem, Col. Johnson devised a springing system which reduced the weight to a minimum. In every tank there are rollers which run on the track as it lays itself on the ground. With all previous British tanks these rollers had been fixed rigidly to the framework of the tank, and the proposal now was that they should be joined in pairs to a bogey which would be connected to the frame through some springing device. To have some form of spring attachment over every bogey would have increased the weight of the tank by several tons. Instead of this the proposal was as follows.

Every bogey should have a pulley mounted on the top and between each pair there was to be a

76   IN THE WAKE OF THE TANK.

pulley fixed to the frame. Figures I and II show diagrammatically the general arrangement. A steel wire rope runs over the bogey pulleys and under the frame pulleys and is kept in tension as shown by a powerful helical spring. In Figure I

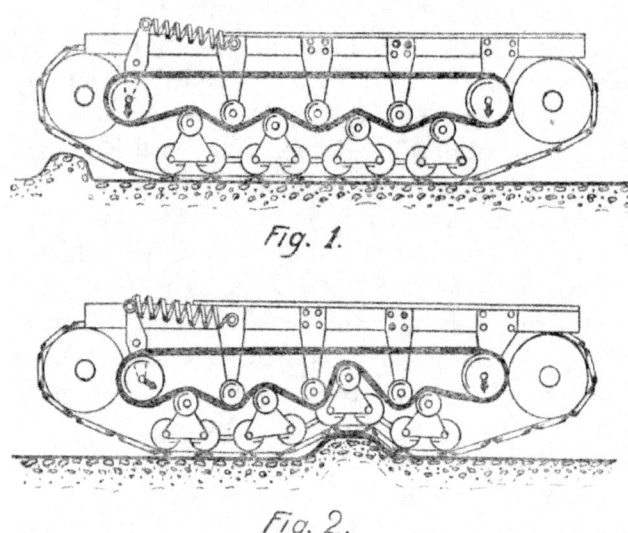

Fig. 1.

Fig. 2.

the tank is running on level ground; hence all the bogeys are on a level with their rollers running on the flat track. In Figure II the tank is passing over a bump and the bogeys are forced up in turn by the bump. This exerts a tension in the cable and so extends the spring. Thus one spring serves as a springing device for all the bogeys of which there might be as many as twelve along one side of a tank; the saving in weight compared with the more normal method of springing each bogey is therefore apparent. In addition, the cable acted as an equaliser; it would often happen that some bogies were mounting a bump while others were falling into small depressions in the ground. By means of the cable, an equalising action would take place and the waste of work in compressing or extending springs would be avoided.

Another interesting point arose over the question of the shape of this machine. This tank had to be able to cross the defences on the enemy front and might have to negotiate difficult obstacles in places. To do so it was thought at that time that a high prow in front was needed. The difficulty with a high prow, however, was that it was almost impossible to provide an unobstructed view from the front of the tank, and as these machines would be working at high speed behind the enemy front good visibility was essential. In the end it was decided that the track should be kept low in front, thereby giving good visibility, but that a high prow should be provided in rear, and that in the event of the tank meeting a difficult obstacle, it would swing right round and take it backwards. We found later that a high prow was not essential and this feature has not been copied in post-war tanks.

All these points and many others were settled at Headquarters, Tank Corps, in France, and then Lieut.-Colonel Johnson was sent home and attached to the Ministry of Munitions to prepare the detail design of the tank.

The work went ahead rapidly; an aeroplane

engine developing 250 h.p. was selected, and the transmission was through epicyclic gears to the driving sprockets on each side. Four speeds were provided, the top and bottom speed being emergency high and low speeds respectively. That is to say top speed was only used on very good going and bottom speed for obstacle crossing, the remaining two being used for normal cross-country work. Another new feature was that the epicyclic gear brake bands were controlled hydraulically, thus eliminating all physical effort required by the driver. The tank weighed 18 tons and the hull was made watertight and had sufficient buoyancy to float in water.

The experimental work was carried out rapidly and made good progress, but the Armistice intervened before the first model was ready. This was, however, completed shortly after the Armistice and the tank went through its preliminary trials. At first all went well; the tank attained a speed of 28 miles an hour on good going on the level and could surmount almost any natural obstacles. It swam across the River Stour near Christchurch, in Hants, repeatedly, plunging in at one bank, propelling itself across with its tracks and climbing out at the other bank with no outside assistance.

Two other models which differed in minor ways were also approaching completion. But although the preliminary trials were so successful and were actually mentioned by Mr. Winston Churchill in Parliament, troubles soon began to materialise. Some of these were put right fairly easily, but others were radical troubles and it eventually became clear that we had tried to aim at too high a specification in one step. It is difficult to say whether a reliable machine of this nature could have been produced in time for our proposed 1919 offensive; the probability is that it would not have materialised. The case, however, did not arise because a little later after the Armistice we settled down to slower and more deliberate research work in this direction; this work is described in the next chapter.

CHAPTER VIII.

EXPERIMENTAL WORK, 1919-1921.

AFTER the Armistice in 1918 we were able to consider the whole question of tank design much more thoroughly and deliberately than had been possible during the stress of war. The types of track and transmission and steering employed on all the war tanks had been practically on the lines of pre-war caterpillar tractors, and we were now able to consider whether we could make fundamental improvements on these rather crude types of track and the methods of steering in use.

The question was very closely bound up with commercial tractor design. Pre-war tractors had only been used for special work, such as hauling timber, and were acknowledged to be very inefficient machines as transport vehicles, but the sight of immense quantities of war stores and supplies being hauled up with tractors across country during an offensive in France excited not only the military mind, as has already been described, but stimulated ideas for colonial development also. It is, of course, a well-known fact that most of our colonies have immense stretches of land which would be of considerable value if only some economic means of transport could be devised to link them with the railways. The land which is easily accessible by road, rail or water is developed at once, but the remainder lies barren until such time as communications are constructed, and both rail and road communications are extremely expensive, and can only be developed slowly. Cross-country tractors would supply the demand, but only if they were efficient, that is to say, they must be capable of transporting goods at a cost not greatly in excess per ton mile of that of a lorry on a hard road. The tanks and tractors that we used during the war worked out at something like five times this cost per ton mile.

This question of transport costs was not merely limited to civilian considerations for the following reason. In peace an army can only afford to maintain a very small proportion of the transport that it needs in war; the remainder must be drawn from civilian resources in the event of war. We have seen that the army needed great numbers of cross-country tractors during the war to maintain an offensive. If, then, these are wanted early in the war they must be in existence and in use for civilian purposes and subsidised and earmarked for mobilisation, because the cost of purchase and upkeep of such large quantities of transport vehicles by the army would be prohibitive in peace time. Hence, although we could afford to purchase and use large quantities of inefficient tractors during the war, we were faced with quite a different proposition when we were considering our peace army after the Armistice and preparation in peace for war.

The solution obviously lay in stimulating the

existing civilian demand for cross-country transport vehicles from the colonies, but it meant the production of an efficient vehicle. All this time our only idea of a cross-country transport vehicle was one that ran on tracks and was practically a tank without a fighting body. If, then, we could produce an efficient tractor it led us straight to an efficient tank also, because although the cost per ton mile is only a small fraction of the total cost in peace or war with a tank, the mere fact of obtaining higher efficiency in cost meant higher speed, longer circuit of action and less maintenance troubles and the possibility of carrying more armour or armament.

A further point arose a little later, when it was found that the type of light draught horse, which we mobilised from civilian sources on the outbreak of the Great War, had been largely replaced by motor vans in England. This meant that our pre-war plans for providing the bulk of our transport for the army in war from horses in civilian use in peace time could no longer be used, and yet we had no suitable tractor or mechanical transport in sight to use in the place of the horses.

Our position as regards this very important experimental work on tank and tractor design after the Armistice was, therefore, as follows. We were experimenting with the Medium D Tank. This was giving a great deal of mechanical trouble; the cable used on the cable suspension had a very short life, the hydraulic control was very unreliable, and many other troubles were experienced. It was not known whether these troubles could be cured by minor alterations or whether the whole tank needed re-design. The tank actually filled our original specification, but the design and constructional work had been rushed through under stress of war and was faulty in many ways; the tank was very unreliable. The main part of our work, however, was directed to an investigation of the problem of producing an efficient track vehicle. All this work was in the hands of a small civilian staff of engineers under Lieut.-Colonel Johnson, who had been working under the Ministry of Munitions and were now transferred to the M.G.O. Branch at the War Office.

It became apparent almost at once that one of the main causes of inefficiency in all track vehicles was due to the method of steering in use. This consisted simply of having a clutch on either side of the machine so that the whole of the engine power could be transmitted to the track on the one or the other side of the tank as desired. When the power was removed from the drive on to one track the tank swung round gradually towards that side. In addition, brakes were provided so that either track could be locked, and when one track was locked the whole machine swung round on its own axis. In either case the machine could only steer by skidding the track round on the ground; there was no question with these tanks of rolling round a bend as one does with a wheeled vehicle. In fact, the method of steering was exactly the same as would exist if the front wheels of a motor car were locked straight ahead and steering was effected by braking on one or the other of the back wheels, so that the car skidded round corners.

This method of steering track vehicles obviously had serious disadvantages. Even a small swing on to a new direction caused loss of speed, while a turn through a right angle absorbed so much power in skidding the track round that it was usually necessary to change down to first gear on the machine. The trouble did not end there, for the stresses set up when swinging and skidding round, meant that an otherwise unnecessarily heavy track and suspension system had to be used to meet these stresses.

The first point, therefore, was to devise some method whereby the track could be laid in a curve and the machine run round on this curve instead of skidding round when steering. New types of track were devised with various types of joint between the plates so as to allow lateral flexibility.

One of the most interesting types was known as the " Snake Track," and is illustrated. It consisted of a type of ball and socket joint between track plates and was very flexible. The rollers were flanged on both sides and ran down this central rail. It was not, however, sufficient to provide a laterally flexible track; unless the bogeys to which the rollers were attached could move sideways and be laid in a curve the tank would not be able to run round the curved track. In this the designs were materially helped by the system of cable suspension already mentioned. The cable could allow the bogies to move laterally as well as up and down. The first experiments consisted merely of fitting tracks with lateral flexibility and bogies which had a certain limited sideways movement. When it was desired to steer, the power was removed from one track in the usual manner, but

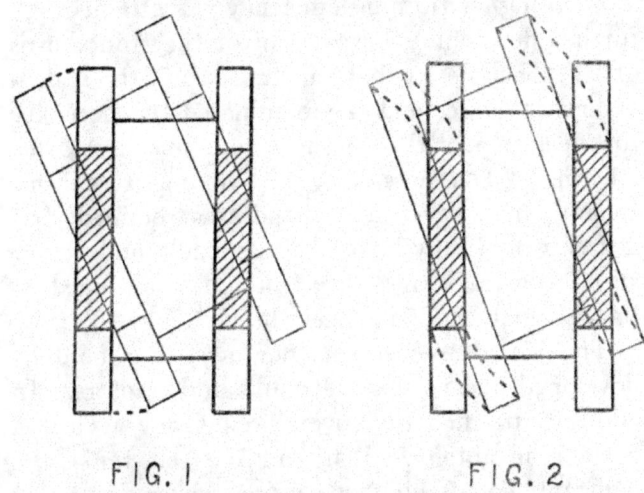

FIG. 1   FIG. 2

instead of this resulting in a skid, the machine would swing round leaving the track in contact with the ground and laying a new portion of track in a curve towards the new alignment.

Figure 1 shows the plan of a tank and the portions of the underside of the track which are resting on the ground are shown shaded. The thin lines show the position of the tank after it has swung through an angle with skid steering. Figure 2 shows a tank fitted with a laterally flexible track and bogies which can move sideways. The thin lines show the tank in the new position and the dotted lines show the underside of the track which is now laying itself in the new direction without any skidding on the ground. In this way it was found that machines could steer through small angles without any loss of momentum, and a much higher running efficiency was attained. A further development was to pivot the front horns of the machine so that the track could be laid in a sharper curve, and this eliminated the necessity for declutching the engine from one track for steering. The possibility of skidding round for turning in a very sharp bend was retained, but as this would only be used occasionally and at low speed the track and suspension did not need to be so heavily built to meet these stresses.

The idea was that this new system should be developed and used on all tanks and tractors. In addition to increased overall efficiency it had a further advantage. With all the war tanks the constant declutching of engine power from one track and the braking on that track for steering caused considerable trouble. Brake bands needed constant adjustment and relining, and the driver had to exert considerable physical effort to work them. With flexible track steering all these troubles would be eliminated. One of the first machines to be built on these lines was known as the Light Infantry Tank. The name did not really mean anything, but the underlying idea was that the machine should be used in countries like

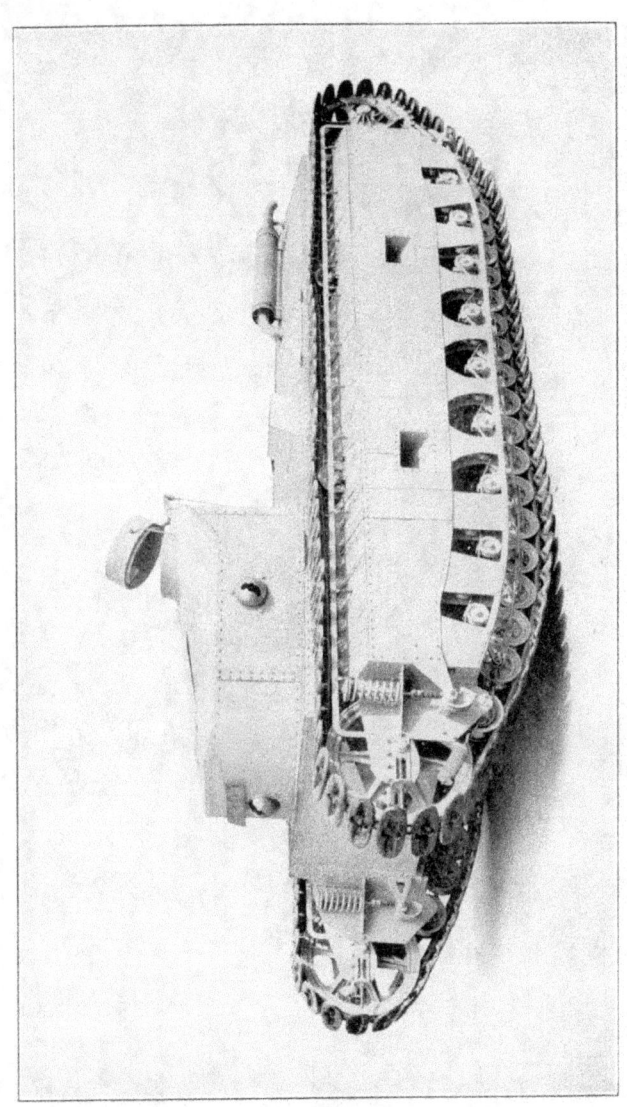

AN EXPERIMENTAL TANK

Built just after the war. The tracks had lateral flexibility for steering and cable suspension. The tank had a maximum speed of 30 m.p.h., and could swim in smooth water, but was rather too lightly constructed and was unreliable.

India, where distances were great. Every effort was made to keep the weight down, and it finally weighed eight tons. It was to be armed with one machine-gun only. The tank put up some remarkable performances. It attained a speed of 30 miles an hour; the body was made watertight and it swam several times across Fleet Pond, near Aldershot. It did not have pivoted horn beams in front, but it had the " Snake Type " of track, cable suspension and bogies with lateral mobility, and it could steer without skidding round a circle with a 30 ft. radius. In petrol consumption per ton mile the machine was at least twice as efficient as any previous tank.

Some tractors were also designed on these lines, but using various types of track, and gave good results. But although striking results were obtained with all these new machines, they one and all proved to be very unreliable. The tracks would come off, rollers would break, the suspension cable gave trouble, etc. What was required was a period of research work to investigate all the points without bothering about any question of whether the chassis would carry a fighting body or be used for a tractor. It was evident that the engineers knew little about the correct design for this new system of steering and suspension. The track also gave trouble. In order to avoid wear and tear, efforts were made to introduce lubricated track joints. The long central tube down the snake track was filled with oil with the idea of lubricating all the ball joints; but grit and sand invariably entered all these joints and made matters worse than with a dry joint.

Without two or three years of work on applied research, it was quite clear that no reliable machines could be constructed incorporating these new ideas and advantages. But it was now two years since the end of the war and the tank battalions were still using the war tanks, which were largely worn out, and were in any case much too slow for the mobile training under peace conditions. It was also very necessary to make a start on mechanizing some of our transport, and artillery traction in particular. These requirements could not wait for several years of research work, with an unknown quantity at the end of it. It was, therefore, decided to construct a tank on normal lines in so far as track design and steering were concerned, but with the greater mobility and reduced trench crossing capacity which was what would be required in the early phases of a war.

As regards transport vehicles, we began to realise that, although a whole track vehicle had been essential for bringing up supplies over the old shell-torn battle-fields in France, these conditions were exceptional, and what we really wanted now was a cross-country lorry, and this was what was wanted by the colonies also. It was, however, still decided to aim at a tank chassis for the new tank, which would be suitable with little alteration for an army tractor.

As regards the Medium D Tank, it was now found that extensive alterations would be needed

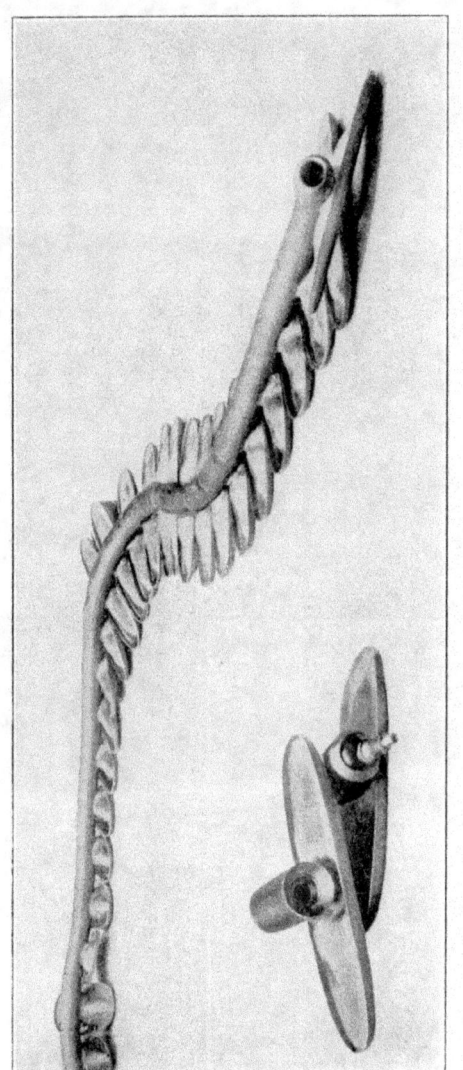

The Snake Track.

to make this tank reliable, and in any case a tank of this nature was no longer needed. That a fast tank was still required for long distance work, delaying enemy main columns, cutting communications, etc., was obvious, but there was now no necessity to hamper design by insisting that such a tank should be able to cross wide trenches. We had been driven to this during the war because our whole front was hemmed in with these trenches, but it was not necessary now. It is true that a long tank is more capable of absorbing obstacles and can travel faster over rough ground than a short tank, and we thought at one time that long tanks would be essential for long distance work, but we found in the end that if the ground is broken, any tank must travel fairly slowly. For long distance work tanks can usually find some sort of track or level ground even if roads are not available, and it is not worth while going to the greatly increased difficulties and cost of constructing long fast tanks to obtain a slightly higher speed over broken ground.

About this time there were considerable reductions in the army due to the necessity for financial economy. The department at the War Office dealing with this work was greatly reduced. To-day we have a representative Mechanical Warfare Board with highly skilled technical officers working on sub-committees, but until this was formed in 1927 the department dealing with this important work was a small one, and unfortunately very few of the officers had any technical knowledge. The reductions included Lieut.-Colonel Johnson and his civilian designers, and with them went most of the work that had been done in an attempt to produce efficient machines. The policy of designing tanks and tractors with normal transmission and steering for our immediate needs was obviously right, but I pressed hard for the retention of the research work on flexible steering and cable suspension. A little work was continued in this direction, but the reductions in staff and absence of technical officers resulted in practically abandoning this work. Whether this system of steering and suspension will ever prove reliable and sufficiently advantageous for adoption is difficult to say; it may be that the best results will eventually be obtained by concentrating on improvements to the skid steering methods, but the possibilities in the former are so great that the research work should have been continued if possible. All this work has now been resurrected, but we have lost six years of research work.

CHAPTER IX.

PROGRESS IN THOUGHT AND DESIGN, 1922-26.

THE decision to produce a tank and tractor using normal methods of transmission and steering led to the construction of the Mark I Vickers Tank and to an Artillery Tractor which became known as the Mark I Dragon. The chassis of each was nearly identical, which was, of course, a great advantage. Although its performance came nowhere near the performances of the experimental machines already referred to, the tank was a great improvement on the war models. It was a fast tank, with a speed of about 20 miles an hour, and was the first fast tank of this nature to be constructed by any nation; in addition it proved to be a reliable machine. The early models used a water-cooled engine, but later an excellent Armstrong-Siddeley air-cooled engine was introduced. The difficulty of carrying and cooling the water in a tank had always been a trouble, and the air-cooled engine solved these difficulties. The introduction of this comparatively untried air-cooled engine was a bold step, and one which was justified by results.

The Mark I Vickers Tank had thin armour which was not proof against ordinary small arm ammunition at all ranges, and thicker armour was used on the Mark II. Full details of the capabilities and armament, etc., of the Mark II Vickers Tank are contained in Appendix I.

Briefly, the tank could cross a 6 ft. clear gap, travel up very steep slopes and cross most natural obstacles. It had a 3-pounder gun in a revolving turret giving all-round fire, and two machine-guns, and weighed a total of 12 tons. The machine was, of course, much too heavy to float and swim across water.

Although mechanically the tank was a considerable success it did not have a good fighting body. The machine-guns could not fire frontally, and there was no place for the Commander of the tank where he could control operations.

The Dragon for artillery traction was also a success mechanically, and the Field Brigade which was equipped with these did some very long marches at comparatively high speeds. There was, of course, no question of a high efficiency as a transport vehicle in cost per ton mile with these vehicles, and no civilian use could possibly have been found for them. No improvement had, therefore, been made in the mobilisation difficulties.

In 1923 the Vickers Tank made its debut in manœuvres at Aldershot. There were then no special anti-tank weapons, and not much attention had been paid to anti-tank training. The result was that in many ways the Vickers Tank dominated the battle-field and caused a certain amount of comment and sensation. During all this time, General (then Colonel) J. F. C. Fuller had been writing about the great future which lay in store

PROGRESS IN THOUGHT AND DESIGN.

for tank warfare, and the arrival of these fast and modern tanks made many officers, who had previously been sceptical, realise that this was not mere speculation into the future. The result was the formation of the Armoured Force on Salisbury Plain. This was the start of the great progress that we have made to-day in modernising our army and bringing it ahead of all other armies in the world.

But many steps occurred between the arrival of the Vickers Tank and the formation of the Armoured Force which played important parts, and these must first be described.

It will be seen that at this time we had only one type of tank in our army, namely the Vickers Tank. When the full capability of this tank was realised, it became generally agreed that it should not be tied to moving in close physical contact with the infantry. Sometimes it was used like cavalry to push out ahead accompanied by lorry-carried infantry, but more usually it was used to attack a position from a flank and thus enable the infantry to capture the position. The tank was, therefore, used rather like the old heavy cavalry. It could not, of course, do everything. We had plenty of commitments in various parts of the world where the work of the infantryman was essential; we could not, therefore, put unlimited money into Vickers Tanks, and, as they were expensive machines, it was obvious that we should have to be contented with comparatively small numbers. There would, therefore, be many cases where infantry would have to fight their way forward without the assistance of Vickers Tanks. And yet the whole teaching of the war was that infantry could not advance against concealed machine-guns until the painfully slow process had been performed of building up the fire plan to put them through under powerful artillery and machine-gun support.

It was with a view to assisting the infantry under these conditions that the experimental construction of some very small cheap tanks was started in 1925. It was also thought that on ground where there was plenty of cover, the enemy might develop a strong defence against Vickers Tanks with concealed anti-tank weapons, and that the larger numbers of these small machines working in close co-operation with the infantry might be even more effective than Vickers Tanks under these conditions. Their use would, of course, be limited to open warfare before the enemy had time to dig continuous trenches. The development and use of these machines is described in detail in Chapter XI, but it is referred to here to make a continuous sequence in describing the progress in thought and design during this period. Briefly, the idea was that the infantry should possess considerable numbers of small cheap tanks which could be paid for financially by a small reduction in infantrymen, and that this would resuscitate their mobility and enable them to advance without delay against inferior forces which were endeavouring to hold them up with machine-guns.

Although the small tank idea might solve the problem of enabling our infantry to retain their

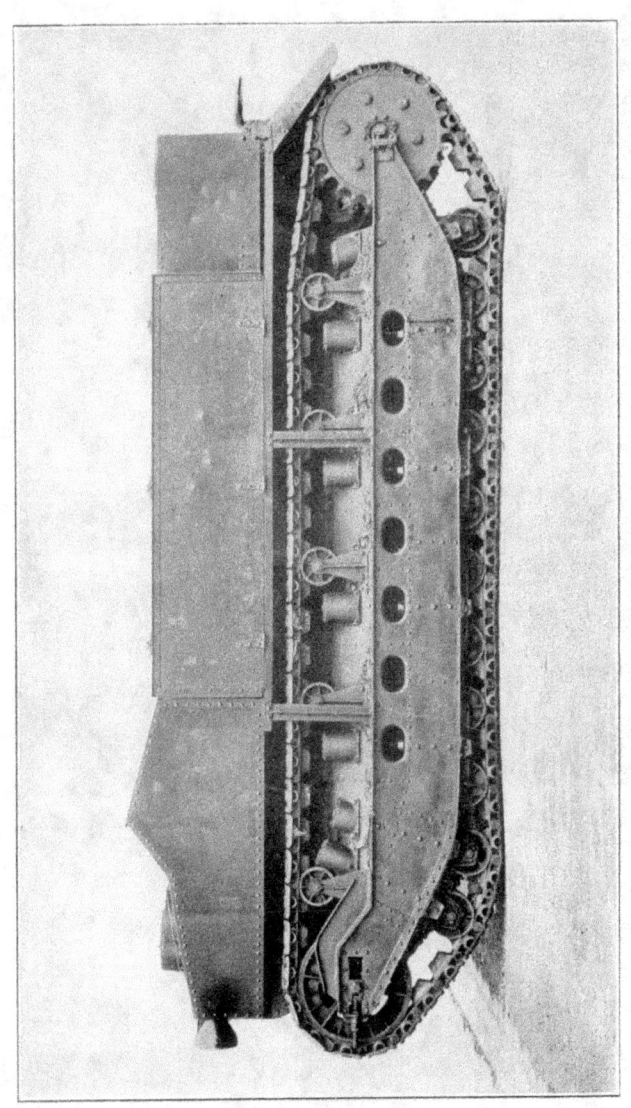

The Dragon Mark II.

The original type of Artillery Tractor; it is now obsolescent.

mobility in open warfare, we still had to consider the case of an enemy remaining on the defensive on perhaps a very wide front and digging himself in. Schemes and exercises which were carried out at the Staff College at Camberley and elsewhere about 1923-1924 brought out very clearly the great defensive power of a modern army using wholesale demolitions and then withdrawing and digging itself in. If the attackers could penetrate this defensive portion of a front quickly, it would usually have led to a decisive result, but there was no known means of doing so.

In Chapter I of this book the necessity for the military authorities having a clear view of what are the main problems of the next war is stressed, the importance being that unless they have this view clearly before them, they will not be able to direct the scientists and engineers towards producing what is required to solve these problems. This question of the rapid penetration through a position which the enemy has prepared for a long delaying action by wholesale demolitions and defences appeared to me to be at any rate one of the main problems of the next war. The effect of the demolitions would be to render the transport problem for supplies and munitions of war very difficult; we were already working at this problem in endeavours to produce economic cross-country lorries or tractors, and a complete account of this work up to the present day appears in Chapter X. But even if we were able to traverse this belt of demolitions by the use of cross-country vehicles, we would still be faced by prepared defences beyond. The enemy would be certain to use large numbers of anti-tank weapons on a defensive position of this nature, and a combination of these and machine-guns would easily hold up our attacks with infantry and tanks until we had gone through the old and lengthy process of collecting masses of artillery to blast our way through his defences.

It was therefore suggested that we should secretly carry out the necessary experimental work and construct a giant tank. The proposal was that this tank should be long enough to cross any trenches which the enemy would be likely to construct, and have armour, proof against all anti-tank weapons up to and including the field gun. It was obvious that we could neither afford, nor would we be allowed, to build any large number of these machines; the proposal was merely that we should complete all the experimental work in peace time. If then a war broke out and there were signs that the enemy might take up the defensive in this way, while he built up an army for offensive operations later, we should at once construct large numbers of these giant tanks. With all the experimental work completed in peace time the output of these tanks could be expected to begin in six months' time. This might appear to be a long delay, but would be far quicker than repeating the Great War process of building up a mass of artillery fire to overcome these defences.

Eventually a heavy tank of this nature was produced, though it was much lighter than the type of tank which some of us had in mind. It was shown to the Dominion Premiers in November, 1926, and photographed by the press so that it is no longer a secret. The tank has a very fine fighting body, with four machine-gun turrets and a central turret for a 3-pounder gun. The Commander of the tank has a command post from which he can control the fire and movement of the tank. The machine has good armour protection and a fair turn of speed. There is, of course, no question of producing any large number of these machines, but the experimental work is being completed so that if we should find ourselves confronted by trench warfare again at some future date we shall be prepared to construct heavy tanks on this or an improved pattern without the tedious delays of preliminary experimental work.

During this time—about 1924-1925—there was no official doctrine on the subject of the use and development of the various types of fighting vehicle. The subject became known as "Mechanicalization," and this unpleasant sounding word was later changed to "Mechanization." The subject was widely discussed, and officers formed their own views on the subject. The position is, of course, quite different to-day; criticism and suggestions are still invited quite freely, but there is now a definite policy governing both the tactical side and the development of new machines.

To sum up, therefore, the position that had been reached by 1926 as regards tanks was briefly as follows. There was the Vickers Tank which had much greater mobility than any previous tanks. They were generally used to attack a position from a flank with the idea of overwhelming it with a surprise attack while the infantry advanced to consolidate the position; but they were also sent off on occasions with lorry-carried infantry and other troops to move round an enemy flank or seize an important position. At the same time a start was being made with the development of small machines with the idea of enabling infantry to advance against concealed machine guns in open warfare without undue delay. Lastly, the design of the heavy tank was in hand with a view to carrying out the experimental work in peace for a tank which might be needed in war if an enemy established himself in a strong defensive position, from which we had to evict him under trench warfare conditions.

By far the greatest interest at this time was centred in the mobile work with Vickers Tanks. The possibility of moving a force 100 miles in 24 hours, of turning the enemy flanks, cutting his communications, etc., was all very attractive. As already stated it was this that led to the formation of the Armoured Force on Salisbury Plain.

During all this time the post-war Tank Corps had been forming and establishing itself at Wool, in Dorset. General Sir H. J. Elles took over command at Wool, and went later to fill the post which was formed of Inspector Royal Tank Corps at the War Office. This post was filled later by Brigadiers C. G. Hankey, G. M. Lindsay, and

K. M. Laird, who controlled in turn the work and training of the Corps. Soon after the war the policy was adopted that we should have Tank Battalions on a scale of one per Division (making four in all) but not forming part of the Division. These were eventually located at Aldershot, Tidworth, Catterick, and Lydd. Armoured car companies remained part of the Tank Corps, though later some cavalry regiments were turned into armoured car regiments. At Wool a very fine system of instruction was established in the tank driving and maintenance schools; the gunnery school at Lulworth Cove became highly developed under Colonel C. N. F. Broad, and a proper system of Tank Corps gunnery was established which did much to change the whole outlook of the army on Tank tactics generally. The post-war Tank Corps attracted a fine type of recruit, and this, coupled with the excellent training that they received at Wool, produced units which could hold their own at work or games with the best units in the army. General Sir John Capper became the first Colonel Commandant of the Royal Tank Corps.

CHAPTER X.

THE DEVELOPMENT OF CROSS-COUNTRY TRANSPORT.

THE attempts to produce an efficient cross-country track vehicle for transport purposes has already been referred to; although this work had a bearing on tank design and was therefore very important, and although we might need some tractors of this nature for special purposes, it was quite clear by 1923 that what we required to fill the bulk of the transport requirements of the army was a cross-country lorry rather than a whole-track vehicle of the tank type. We wanted to be able to travel cross-country and cross small natural obstacles, but not the shell-torn ground of the Great War. It was far better to have a really mobile lorry at a reasonable price and expend a little work on easing the passage over difficult obstacles, than have a slower and much more expensive machine which could cross almost anything. The former also held out the only chance of adoption for civil use and the consequent advantages to the army.

Right from the start the R.A.S.C. had been far-sighted enough to put their faith in a wheeled cross-country lorry, and about this time they produced a Thornycroft lorry with drive on all four wheels. The vehicle, which was a tractor more than a lorry, was known as the Hathi, and had large size pneumatic tyres. It also had a winding

THE HATHI.

The first cross country lorry or tractor on wheels. It had four-wheel drive on large pneumatic tyres.

gear driven off the engine, and to negotiate a steep or difficult obstacle the Hathi passed over first and then wound the gun or trailer across with a steel wire rope on the winding gear. It was a remarkable machine and stood some severe tests, and if the army had not still been somewhat over-concerned about crossing the exceptionally bad ground which we had seen in France, the Hathi would have had a better reception. Its chief drawback was that on wet slippery clay soil and mud, wheel slip was apt to occur rather easily and hold up the machine.

In competition with the Hathi a new type of lorry was now developed known as the half-track lorry. This was an ordinary commercial lorry, but using a short track instead of the back wheels. The advantage of this lorry was that it used commercial parts very largely. There were two types; one used a steel track and the other a rubber track. Although other firms made a few of these lorries, the chief manufacturers were Morris Commercial, who produced a 30-cwt. lorry fitted with steel tracks provided by Roadless Traction, Ltd., while the Crossley firm produced a 30-cwt. vehicle using the Kegresse rubber half-track. Both machines, and particularly the latter, put up good cross-country performances and a fair number were used by the army in experimental units, and many of the Crossley cross-country lorries are still in use. They were a great improvement on the whole-track vehicles. Their chief disadvantage was that their performance on roads was not very economical; there was also a good deal of trouble with slip on the friction drive of the rubber tracks, while the steel tracks had a comparatively short life in sand and grit. An improved type of Kegresse rubber track is now available which overcomes some difficulties but does not materially improve the road efficiency.

In the meantime, the R.A.S.C. were developing a lorry with two back axles and two pairs of back driving wheels. The idea was of French origin, the Renault firm having produced a cross-country motor car in this way. The R.A.S.C., however, developed the idea and introduced a clever device to take up the torque reaction on the back axles.

The six-wheel lorry is practically a normal lorry but with a second back axle located in rear of the normal back axle, the drive being taken through

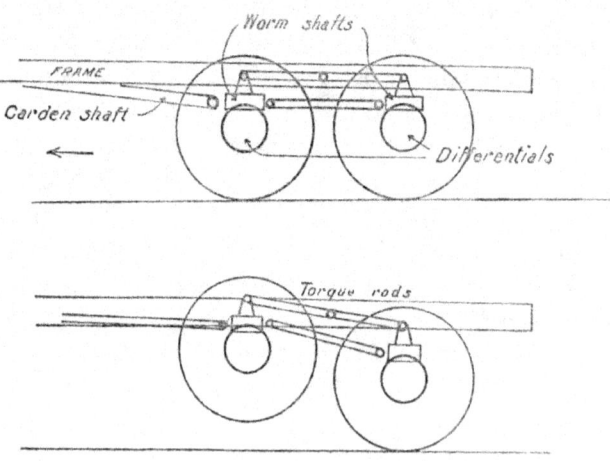

Worm shafts remain parallel.

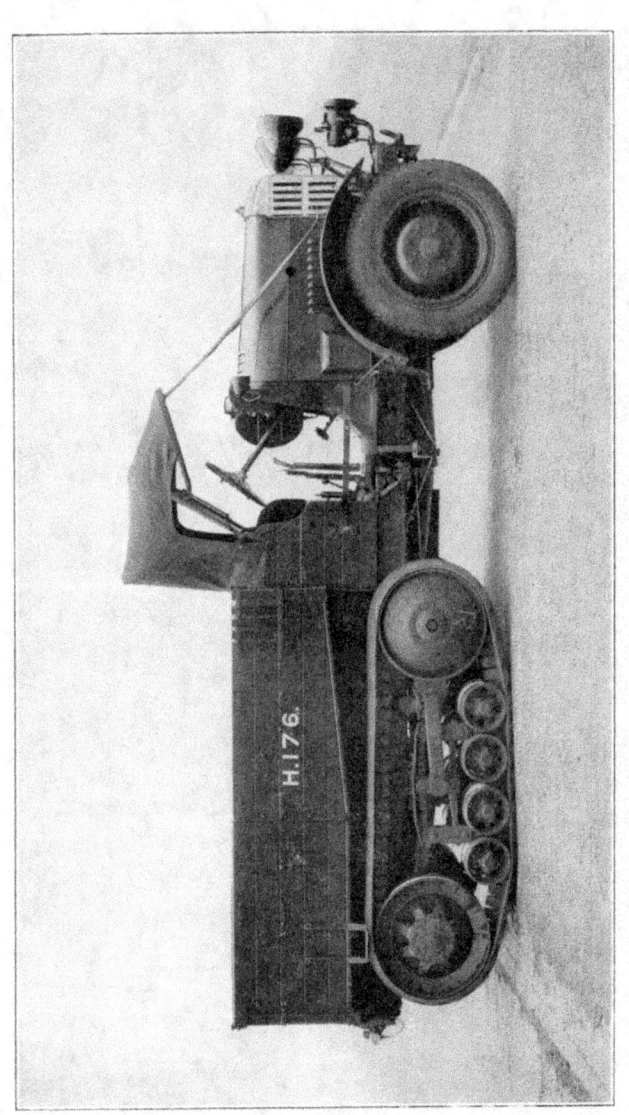

The Crossley Half-Track Lorry.

A typical lorry of the half-track type; these lorries had a good cross-country performance, but were not adopted commercially.

the worm shaft of the front differential to the rear worm shaft. The figure shows the idea diagrammatically. If the vehicle is being driven in the direction shown by the arrow, the housings of the differentials tend to revolve in a clockwise direction due to the torque reaction. In addition to causing sudden excess stresses, this movement tends to make the back pair of wheels dig in to soft ground while the front wheels rise and wheel-slip then occurs. The torque rods were, therefore, introduced. These rods are held by universal joints at each end, and anchor the differential casing to the frame, so that although the axles have free up-and-down movement the worm shafts must remain parallel. There are some engineers who consider that the advantage of these torque rods is more theoretical than practical. The system has, however, been generally adopted, and large numbers of firms are now supplying six-wheel lorries built on this system.

The advantages of the six-wheel lorry are, of course, obvious. The whole lorry can be the normal commercial product of the firm with the addition of a second back axle. The extra fitments for springing and the drive to the rear axle are simple additions, and any firm producing ordinary lorries could very soon be producing six-wheel lorries in war. The lorry has a good road performance, and a remarkable cross-country capacity. Special chains can be placed round the two back wheels to obtain extra adhesion when required for crossing obstacles or short lengths of boggy ground. They are being made in both the 30-cwt. and 3-ton class by a large number of firms in England. The heavier types are in actual commercial use at home for buses and load carrying; the extra load that can be carried paying for the cost of the second axle. The 30-cwt. lorry has made little progress commercially at home, but an increasing number are being asked for and used abroad, the reason being that the four-wheel 30-cwt. lorry can carry the load on good roads and no advantage is gained in this case by using a second back axle.

Many tests were carried out between 1924 and 1926 to compare the performance of the six-wheel lorry and the half-track vehicle. Such tests are, however, apt to become spectacular stunts. Certain types of boggy ground could be found which the half-track vehicle could negotiate and over which the six-wheeler failed, and of course the whole-track vehicle, such as the Dragon, could surmount obstacles and pass over ground which the lorries could not look at. This type of ground could, however, nearly always be avoided in war and especially in mobile warfare.

Many experiments are being tried to improve still further the obstacle-crossing capacity of the wheeled lorries. Some have a drive provided for the front wheels, and this considerably increases their capabilities in this direction. Another series of experiments which is being tried is the use of the Pavesi system for wheeled vehicles. By this system the drive is taken to both front and rear axles and the axles can rotate laterally, quite freely

The Morris Six-Wheel 30-cwt. Lorry.

and independently of each other. In this way the wheels at the end of each axle press equally on the ground over which the vehicle is passing, however uneven it may be. A tractor with a pair of wheels at the end of each axle is being tried using this system; this vehicle has thus eight driven wheels and can cross surprising obstacles. But all these special vehicles are entirely non-commercial, and there is little chance of their commercial adoption. They must, therefore, remain very expensive, and no facilities will exist in peace time for large scale production of these vehicles in war.

In the meantime the six-wheel lorry is being used more extensively in the army every day and is now firmly established. The development of this lorry and the way in which commercial firms have been persuaded to adopt it, is a fine piece of work and has done much for the progress which we are making in putting the army on a more mobile basis. Although all this work is now controlled by the Mechanical Warfare Board, with its expert advisers, the development of the six-wheel lorry was originally launched by a small band of enthusiasts in the R.A.S.C., with little outside support or encouragement.

So far we have discussed the transport vehicles in daily use in the army or under trial, but there is another line of thought which has existed ever since the war and which is now beginning to take shape. There is at present a great demand from the colonies for transport vehicles that can do comparatively short runs from outlying land to the nearest railway, and for this, as we have seen, the six-wheel lorry at present offers the best chance of success; but there is also the question of developing land which lies at a great distance from any railway, and which would have to wait a long time before the capital was available for railway construction. For this purpose the small load carrying vehicles are unsuitable, and what is required is a cross-country train. This had been discussed by some of us who were interested in these problems for many years. It has been pointed out that the world's demand for transportation on land appears to be insatiable. The whole world may be passing through a period of depression in commerce, but in spite of this it is quite certain that more cars and lorries will be sold next year than last year, and this demand for transport on land appears to have been increasing quite steadily throughout all times.

Viewed from a general point of view there are five known methods of transport in the world to-day.

A ship has two-dimensional movement and can move to any desired point, it can also save costs by carrying a very large load, in fact, the larger the cargo the smaller are the transport costs. Against this a ship has constantly to displace a mass of water as it moves forward. This causes very little loss of efficiency at low speeds, but the loss increases very rapidly as the speed increases. High speed is not, however, an important feature in most transport work.

The Overall Chain which enables these lorries to surmount obstacles and greasy banks.

An aeroplane has three-dimensional movement and is quite unrestricted in that way, and can attain a comparatively high speed with no loss in economic efficiency. On the other hand, the constant fight against gravity limits the size of the load; the larger the aeroplane the larger the proportion of weight required for engines and gear to keep the aeroplane in the air and the smaller is the proportion of useful load. This is a very serious handicap economically, and practically limits aeroplane transport to light loads where high speed is required. The possibilities of airship transport commercially are too unknown at present to discuss, but in principle they avoid this particular failing of the aeroplane.

On land we have the remaining three methods of transport, namely, by road, rail and cross-country. Road and rail transport both suffer from being one-dimensional movement, and both have the great handicap of requiring an enormous capital outlay on the communications before they can start operating. The railway can take heavy loads efficiently and at a fair speed, and is, therefore, more economical than the road, which is limited to vehicles carrying a few tons at a time. If special roads were built to take very powerful lorries carrying or towing heavy loads, the transport costs would fall, but the capital cost on the road would be prohibitive. Against this, cross-country transport has none of these failings. By cross-country transport is meant a mechanical means of taking heavy loads across country without the capital outlay on a made road, but the vehicles would keep to a track along which obstacles had been removed. This form of transport has two-dimensional movement because tracks can be picked out to any desired point within limits, and there is nothing to prevent very large loads being carried, if this type of train is properly designed.

During the war we had suggested that we should have some wagons made and mounted on tracks so that we could tow up large quantities of stores, like a train behind a tank or powerful tractor, to meet our maintenance difficulties, but, owing to the state of the ground on all battlefields at the time, it was thought better to keep to individual tractors carrying or towing small loads.

After the war Lieut.-Colonel Johnson designed some plans in outline for cross-country trains of this nature, and the problem has been discussed at various times. More recently the problem has taken a more concrete form, and the Colonial Office is investigating the question as a result of a demand from the Sudan.

The general idea might be something in the nature of a 100-ton train travelling at five miles an hour. At a low speed like this there is no reason why a powerful tractor on tracks should not tow wagons carrying a total load of this nature quite economically, and, although the running costs would be greater than that of a railway train, they might well be less than the running costs plus interest and depreciation on the capital outlay of a newly constructed railway. The low speed would be essential for economical running, but for transporting most of the exports of a country, a high speed is not essential.

If this type of cross-country train is developed commercially, it will have a great bearing on military operations. Plans which would be impossible to-day because of transportation difficulties, would become quite feasible with the advent of cross-country trains, and this commercial development will be of great interest to us.

CHAPTER XI.

SMALL TANKS.

EVER since the Armistice in 1918 proposals had been made that some small experimental tanks should be constructed, mainly with a view to their being used as scouts for the larger and more powerful tanks. Captain O. S. Penn, who had served in the Tank Corps during the war and was employed for a time on design work with tanks after the war, had produced outline designs of a few types of small vehicles of this nature. The idea at the time was that they should have little or no armour and depend for protection on their speed. A little later, at the Staff College, Camberly, I stressed the importance of having small machines of this type, but more with a view to having them properly armoured, and used to assist infantry. This led to discussion but nothing further. Towards the end of 1924 Colonel Karslake spoke to me at the War Office, and said that he could not understand why we did not make small cheap machines to assist the infantry even if we had faster and more powerful machines as well for use in a more independent rôle. This led me to revive the old proposals; I was not at the time officially connected with any work for tanks, but I knew that the original proposals had been turned down, and thought that the quickest method of progress would be to produce a working model which officers would be able to see.

The first step was to obtain a clear idea of the use to which this small tank was to be put, and then to prepare a specification to which the construction of the machine should aim.

Tanks had so far taken the form of rather big and expensive machines. For instance, it was estimated that the cost of purchase and maintenance of a section of five Vickers Tanks came to about the same as the maintenance of a company of infantry. This was calculated on the basis that a tank should have a life of five years and that the capital cost should be spread over those years. In other words, the 150 personnel in an infantry company balanced in cost the tank crews of 5 tanks (25 personnel) with the addition of 5 tanks and the extra personnel who belong to a Tank Section. Hence, if we wanted to produce a large number of tank units, the only way of paying for them financially was a large reduction in infantry units. There are, however, so many commitments in the British Army which can only be met by the use of infantrymen that a large reduction of this arm was not possible. If, however, we could produce a fighting machine that would help the infantry forward and was so cheap that it could be paid for by the replacement of one or two infantrymen, then it was quite another proposition.

The Vickers Tanks would in many cases be used on the flanks or for special missions, but even if they were used to assist the advance of infantry battalions in close country their efficiency was in doubt, owing to the rapid advances that were being made in anti-tank weapons, and it was thought that if a comparatively small number of Vickers Tanks were used in close country they would suffer very heavy casualties from these weapons. The normal method which the soldier has always used to avoid casualties from fire on the move has been to use dispersion, e.g. the continuous line of advancing infantry, used against muskets, had to be dispersed to men extended at 10 or even 20 yards to face rifle or machine-gun fire. Hence in this case the solution might lie in dispersing the very expensive Vickers Tank into, say, fifteen or twenty smaller tanks.

With these views in mind it seemed to me that the following specification should be aimed at for the first experimental model.

1. To be able to traverse any ground and cross any natural ditch or bank that is likely to be met.
2. Speed on good ground or roads 15 m.p.h. on the level.
3. Speed on rough or bumpy ground 3 to 4 m.p.h.
4. Climb a slope of 1 in 1.
5. To use an ordinary motor car engine of about 20 h.p., and the component parts of the tank to be ordinary commercial parts as far as possible, so that they could be obtained in large quantities for war.

6. To be proof from the front and flanks against small arm armour-piercing bullets.

7. Armament to be one light automatic rifle.

The first model was now made as a private experiment in my workshop at my house in Camberley. As a first trial it was made to hold one man only, who should both drive the machine and fire the automatic. The work was started in February and completed by August, 1925. Many demonstrations were then given, and they caused considerable interest and discussion. The machine came fairly near to meeting the above specification. It could cross most natural obstacles that would be met when travelling cross-country; large irrigation ditches or strong hedges, and, of course, steep nullahs, such as exist in India, would stop the machine quite easily, but there are usually crossing places available through hedges or over wide ditches, and, generally speaking, the machine had a good cross-country capability. The speed of 15 miles an hour on the level was obtained, and the machine was made almost entirely of ordinary commercial component parts of motors, with the addition of a pair of tracks.

The question of capital cost and maintenance now arose. It was estimated that a machine of this type would cost £400. If it lasted for five years, which was not an unreasonable proposal, the capital cost could be taken as £80 a year for a rough calculation. For running expenses, if we assumed 2,000 miles a year, which was much more than the Vickers Tanks were allowed to do, the cost should not exceed £30 a year. Hence the total annual cost of the machine would be about £110 a year. These figures were laughed at and stated to be ridiculous at the time by many people who considered that they had been put far too low, but they have not turned out to be very far astray to-day for the machines that are now carrying out this work.*

This machine had made the soldier into a " mechanical infantryman," or " mechanical knight," and this idea of the one-man tank caught the imagination and was freely discussed in the press; in particular Capt. B. H. Liddell Hart was one of the first to write and suggest great future prospects for machines of this nature. There were, however, many arguments in favour of putting two men in each machine. Financially, it worked out like this. If we took the figure of £110 per annum for one machine the cost was practically the same as that of one infantryman (£120 a year). If, therefore, we replaced two infantrymen in a battalion by one of these tanks with one man inside the cost to the State was the same. If, however, we put two men inside the tank it meant replacing three men in the unit by one machine. Looked at another way, for the same cost we could have 3 one-man tanks or 2 two-man tanks, and for many purposes in war we wanted as many of these small machines as we could get.

---

* This work is now being carried out by " in-fighter armoured machine gun carriers," which will be referred to in Chapter XV.

The Original One-man Tank which started the train of thought towards "Armoured machine-gun carriers" and "In-fighters," which are described in Chapter XVII. Major-General Fuller is on the right.

There was no great difficulty in both driving the machine and firing an automatic rifle. The same thing is done in a single-seater fighter in the air, and a cavalryman rides his horse while fighting. However, after some discussion it was considered that the strain on a single man would be too great, and that these machines were to have two men, one to drive and the other to shoot.

No one had any very clear idea at the time as to how many of these machines an infantry battalion should possess. We would, of course, have to try out a few at a time and see how they worked. As an object to aim at, however, in the distant future, I wrote several articles that appeared later in the *Army Quarterly* and other journals, and argued the position as follows.

Assuming that we had obtained the ideal machine which could fulfil our specification and at the above cost, then we can take a battalion at 1,000 strong and change it into a battalion of mechanical infantry 500 strong mounted in 250 of these machines. If now we take an infantry brigade, mechanize the infantry in this way, and add to it a normal proportion of mechanized artillery and other necessary troops, we get what we might call a modern mechanized division, because this would be quite as large a mechanized force of all arms as any commander could control. Thus our expeditionary force could be changed from four divisions to twelve mechanized divisions at no increase of cost.

It may at first sight seem that a battalion of

250 of these small tanks would be quite uncontrollable, but it should be made clear that the machines merely had armour on the front and sides and the men could see signals and be controlled when moving forward in extended order in much the same way as infantry are controlled. The mobility of a mechanized division should be at least four times that of an ordinary division. If the division advanced 80 miles it would need 30 three-ton lorries to fill it up again with petrol and oil, and this is not an excessive number of lorries, so the mobility of the division should not be unduly hampered by administrative difficulties.

In action a mechanized division would act very much like armoured cavalry. To hold a position the men would dismount and use their weapons on the ground; large numbers of men are not needed for defence, and, in any case, we still had 500 per battalion, and no horse holders would be needed with these machines. If wooded or mountainous country was met, the men would again dismount and fight on foot.

It might be argued that there was no point in mechanizing the whole of the infantry, and that a number of these machines in each battalion was all that was required. This, however, would leave the division with its present very low mobility. Some of the most successful armies in past history have consisted entirely of cavalry, every man being mounted, and great results were obtained by the use of their mobility. It was also argued that this mobility could more easily be obtained by putting the infantry into lorries. If these are unarmoured most of the mobility is lost because, owing to their vulnerability, the ground must be searched for isolated enemy machine-guns before they can advance. This reduces the speed of advance to about five miles an hour if there is any chance of meeting machine-guns which have been pushed forward for this purpose. If the lorries are armoured they are very expensive and an attractive target for air bombing. By moving the men in these little two-man tanks, they were proof against stray machine guns, they could deploy without delay, and they could disperse to avoid casualties from artillery fire or bombing.

These views were, of course, only a suggestion for something to look to in the distant future. The general proposal was that the whole of the infantry of the regular army was to become mechanized infantry. For a Continental war we would thus have 12 of the new proposed mechanized divisions which would undoubtedly be of far greater value than the four existing divisions. Their mobility would enable them to concentrate rapidly on the enemy flank, and in attack it was difficult to imagine what sort of defence the enemy could put up in mobile warfare against such large numbers of fighting vehicles. In fact, the action of this small mechanized army in a Continental battle might be decisive. There would, of course, be plenty of work for which ordinary infantry would be required, and for which it would be wasteful to use the highly-trained mechanized infantry of our regular army. But this work, such as the defence of portions of the front which were on the defensive and the guarding of lines of communication, could be carried out easily enough by hastily raised infantry units.

For our work abroad the case was not so easy to argue. In many parts the only man who can fight, is the man on his feet, but we still had 500 men per battalion for this work, and they could be concentrated at the desired place much more rapidly owing to their mobility. In some of our foreign possessions we have very long frontiers, and the only possible defence is offensive action against an invader, for which these small fighting vehicles would be very suitable. For the static defence abroad of such places as oil depôts and coaling stations the mechanized infantry would be wasted, but our highly trained regular army should not be used for such work, which should be left to local troops or volunteers.

It does not, therefore, seem impossible that some scheme of this nature should eventually materialise. The infantryman is now the only man in the civilised world who walks to his work, and some scheme whereby the mobility of the whole army is increased is bound to come in time. That the above proposals will come true in detail is unlikely because military prophecies are nearly always wrong, but it is essential to consider future developments or else there can be no general guiding policy for the present.

A further point of interest in connection with

SMALL TANKS.

this idea of mechanized infantry was the possibility of using them for landing operations. This type of operation, with which the British Army is so often concerned, receives much study; and shortly after the trials with the first experimental model at Camberley, I arranged to take it down and carry out a private trial with the Royal Navy at Gosport. They very kindly assisted in every way, and prepared a boat with a drawbridge for a landing trial. The tank was put into the boat, which was then brought on to the shore and beached, and the drawbridge was at once dropped into the shallow water. The tank had the engine running and mounted at once on to the drawbridge and plunged over it into the water. It then scrambled through the water and up over a muddy beach on to firm land in less than a minute. The trial showed clearly that machines of this nature would be of the greatest assistance in landing operations, and would often make for success where the landing of unarmoured men would be quite impossible.

In the meantime official action was being taken in the development of these machines. The Morris Commercial firm agreed to make some models based on the original model and using Morris parts. Fortunately at this stage some competition came in from two engineers, Messrs. Carden and Loyd, who were in charge of a large garage in London. Mr. Carden had felt for a long time that some means of mobility should be given to the infantryman, and had made a very small low track machine for carrying one man. The idea was that he should travel in practically a lying-down position and should be taken rapidly forward along the ground and be comparatively inconspicuous. The machine was unarmoured. Mr. Carden had made an experimental model and tried it, but had not pursued the matter. When, however, the Press reported the trials of the one-man tank, Mr. Carden asked to be allowed to produce machines of his own design. His first models were still on the idea of a very low inconspicuous machine without armour and were not a great success. Later, however, he produced a two-man machine with armour protection, and with the same idea as the machines that were now being made by the Morris Commercial firm.

It was now 1926, and it was decided that a number of these machines should be ordered for use with the Mechanized Force* which was to be formed on Salisbury Plain. These machines were called Tankettes at this time, and they were required to act as scouts for the force; this was not the type of work for which they had been designed, and they had neither the speed nor the necessary all-round armour protection for this work; they were, however, the only machines which could be made available in the time. Eight Morris and eight Carden machines were ordered, and were used with the force in both 1927 and 1928. The Morris machines were strong and reliable; they were kept running by their crews with only a very small number of spare parts, and

---

* This Force is described in Chapter XIII.

were actually running better in 1928 than 1927, in spite of the heavy work they had done; they had, however, many disadvantages for this type of work. The Carden machines were a Mark IV model, and much improved over earlier types; they were rather weak in some ways, and consumed large numbers of spare parts; they had, however, many advantages over the Morris machine. All this time Mr. Carden was producing new models, and eventually evolved the Mark VI, which was an excellent machine. The Morris machine never got beyond the Mark I. The firm were too busy with their commercial work to carry out a long series of experimental trials, and I had my own work to do, and could not continue indefinitely with this work as a spare-time hobby, and the Morris machine died out.

About this time it became clear that two types of machine were required. A Mechanized or Armoured Force needed fast machines, and as they would be used out ahead as scouts they required all-round protection and all-round fire, if possible. On the other hand the machine for fulfilling the original idea of assisting the infantry did not need great speed, and there were many advantages in having a shield only for giving protection from the front and flanks. It was, therefore, decided that further experimental work should be carried out on two lines; i.e. the development of a fast light tank for scouting work, and a slower and less conspicuous machine for work with infantry. The latter became known as the Armoured Machine Gun Carrier and the word "Tankette" was abolished. The Mark VI Armoured Machine Gun Carrier was produced by Mr. Carden in 1928, and proved remarkably successful; great ingenuity was displayed in the mechanical design which showed a wide knowledge of mechanical engineering; the army owes much to Mr. Carden, and will probably owe still more to him in the future. Further work with the Light Tank and the Armoured Machine Gun Carrier is described in Chapters XVI and XVII.

The Carden-Loyd Armoured Machine-gun Carrier.

CHAPTER XII.

THE PASSAGE OF TANKS OVER OBSTACLES.

THE passage of tanks over obstacles was naturally a very important subject for us to study at Headquarters Tank Corps, and the whole of our work in this direction, together with the progress that has been made since the war, will be dealt with in this chapter. Although our war tanks had considerable powers of overcoming obstacles, there were many common and natural obstacles which would hold them up.

The first bridging device which we had to consider was not, however, connected with the passage of the tank, but of the supporting infantry, across the obstacle. Rumours were in existence that the enemy would fill his forward trenches with barbed wire before we attacked with tanks and hold a line a little further back. In that way the tanks would pass over these trenches without crushing the barbed wire, which would remain a serious obstacle to the infantry supporting the tanks. It would have been an easy and somewhat obvious step for the enemy to carry this out, and so provide himself with a concealed obstacle, but he never did so. We could not, however, foretell this, and we took the precaution of carrying out experimental work to provide a means of passage for the infantry across an obstacle of this nature. The solution was the carriage of a long light bridge in the form of an infantry trench board on the tail of a tank, as shown in the sketch.

The bridge was kept in this position by a thin rope, as shown. The idea was that the tank would cross the trench that was filled with wire, and, as soon as it was across, the rope would be released from inside the tank. The bridge would then fall across the trench, and the hinged junction at the

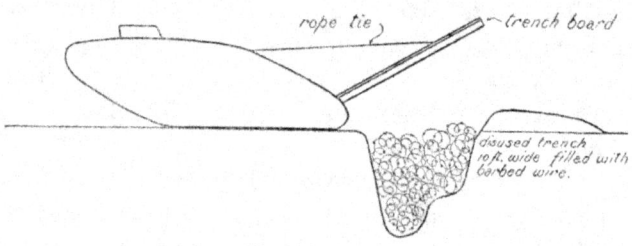

lower end was so arranged that this would then disengage, leaving the bridge across the gap. The necessary experiments were carried out and a few models made. The design was kept very simple, and large numbers could have been made and fitted to tanks at short notice if the necessity had arisen. This is yet another of the many experiences from the war that has by now been forgotten by most people, but might easily arise again in a future war.

The next type of bridge which we developed was a device to enable medium tanks to follow heavy tanks across very wide trenches. It will be remembered that we had to introduce lighter and faster tanks, which were known as medium tanks, for the semi-mobile warfare beyond the main trench systems. These wide trenches could have been ramped down or filled in for the passage of medium tanks, but this would have meant delay, and it might also have been desired to let loose medium tanks behind the enemy main trench systems before they were entirely captured, in which case it might not have been possible for men to work there in the open. To meet this demand a bridge in the form of a sledge was designed. This consisted essentially of two steel joists as main girders and sufficient bracing between them to hold them in their right positions; light timber planks were placed across these girders. The bridge was 20 ft. long, and could be towed quite easily by a heavy tank; the tank would cross the wide trench and the bridge followed across without any difficulty. When the bridge was spanning right across the trench, the towing attachment could be released from inside the tank, leaving the bridge across the trench. The medium tanks could then pass over on the timber planks. These planks were really only there to give confidence and to prevent slipping between the steel tracks of the tank and the joists, but the tank had to steer fairly closely over the joists, which were located just under each tank track of the tanks. A few of these bridges were made for trials, but by the time that we had any number of medium tanks in France the conditions of warfare had changed, and we were no longer faced with these very wide trenches along the whole front. These bridges were, therefore, never used.

After the Battle of Cambrai, the necessity arose for a bridging device to enable tanks to cross canals at the locks. It was evident that the enemy would now make all possible use of anti-tank obstacles, and the numerous canals that existed would often give him a natural line of obstacles. These canals, however, had locks at various intervals, which were all about 20 ft. wide in the clear gap, with strong concrete walls each side. Moreover the approaches on each side of the lock were usually fairly easy, so that they were ideal places at which to bridge the canal for the passage of tanks. It was, however, essential that this bridging should be done by some device attached to or pushed by tanks, because that was the only means whereby the gap could be spanned under fire in the forefront of the battle, thus enabling tanks to lead the assault across the obstacle.

The problem was an interesting one and we started working on it, and devised a bridge carried in front of a tank like a raised bowsprit, which could be lowered down across the gap, working entirely from inside the tank. At this time, however, it became clear that, although we had plenty of sappers* at Tank Corps Headquarters or in the

---

* *Note.*—The following were among the R.E. Officers closely connected with the early days of tanks:—
General Sir E. D. Swinton, who initiated the whole movement.
General Sir H. J. Elles, who commanded the Tank Corps throughout the war.
Lt.-Col. R. C. R. Hill, who commanded one of the early battalions.
Capt. G. Le Q. Martel, who was Brigade-Major when Tank Corps Headquarters were first formed.
Later, General Sir John Capper became Director-General for Tanks at home, and Major S. H. Foot was on his Staff.

Tank Corps, we should now ask for assistance from the Engineer-in-Chief at G.H.Q. This came at once, and Major C. E. Inglis was sent to see us and discuss our problems.

As regards general bridging requirements, the Engineer-in-Chief had very wisely been collecting a great quantity of girder bridges at R.E. Parks to meet the demand which he knew would arise as soon as we advanced towards Germany. This work had been started as early as 1915, and Major Inglis, who was an authority on civil bridge building, was one of the engineers called in to assist with the design of these girder bridges, which had to be designed, so that they were easily portable and quickly launched; incidentally, this work proved to be a wise and necessary precaution. Though the shipping space which all these bridges occupied in transit from England to France was grudgingly given, and sometimes refused, our army was fully equipped when the great advance came, and a long way ahead of other armies in this respect, and our supply of bridges which had been collected through all these years proved to be just sufficient to keep pace with the demands. The main point with which we were concerned was that all, or as many as possible, of these bridges should be made capable of taking our heavy tanks. A good many alterations were necessary. Some of the girder bridges were too narrow to take tanks unless their sponsons were removed or closed in. This was obviously undesirable. In other cases transoms had to be strengthened. This work proceeded at once, and in addition Major Inglis was instructed to design a heavy Inglis Tubular Bridge which should be specially suitable for our heavy tanks.

Major Inglis was also to take over the experimental work on the tank bridge for crossing at locks over canals under fire, and this became known as the Tank Canal Lock Bridge. He was also to investigate the possibility of mounting girder bridges on idle tracks, with a view to pushing them cross-country by means of tanks, and straight across river obstacles without delay; all this work went ahead very fast in England.

Towards the end of the war it became clear that the bridging of tank obstacles would be a matter of primary importance as we advanced, and that we would only be able to do this rapidly in some cases if we used the mechanical power of the tank. Three Tank Bridging Battalions were, therefore, formed at Christchurch, in Hants, in October, 1918, and as I had been closely connected with the design side of our various requirements at H.Q. Tank Corps in France, I was sent home to command one of these battalions and to assist in this new work. I only arrived there, however, about a week before the Armistice, and shortly afterwards the other two battalions were disbanded leaving mine there alone. A little later this battalion was reduced to an experimental establishment of which I was put in charge.

The bridging battalions were each to have been equipped with 12 of the new Inglis Tubular Girder

PASSAGE OF TANKS OVER OBSTACLES. 129

Bridges and 48 tanks fitted with the canal lock bridge made to a new design which had been prepared by Major Inglis, and it was our duty, as the experimental establishment, to complete the trials with this new equipment.

The tubular bridge was capable of taking tanks weighing 35 tons across a clear gap of 100 ft.; it was easy to transport and rapid in erection, and, although Major Inglis had to prepare the design in a minimum of time, no faults that mattered came to light during the trials. Special large pontoons were also provided, and when used in combination with the girder work enabled a long floating bridge to be constructed that could take heavy tanks across a wide water obstacle. This work of bridging for 35-ton tanks presented difficult problems; it was far in excess of any loads which had ever been previously considered for military bridges; there is, however, little doubt that if the war had continued these bridging battalions could have competed successfully with the problem with this equipment.

The design of the tank canal lock bridge prepared by Major Inglis worked well, but it had also been done hastily, and now that we were able to spend more time on it, we produced a new design which was worked hydraulically.

The sappers in our experimental establishment were good tradesmen, and we were, therefore, in a position to forge ahead with this experimental work. As a result of our experience with tanks, we were determined to use engine power in every possible way to assist us in our R.E. work. The only tanks existing at that time in any numbers were the heavy tanks, and until such time as more mobile tanks were available, our proposal was that all Field Companies should have one section of these tanks to assist them in their work by using its mechanical power. If tanks increased in proportion to the rest of the army a larger proportion of more mobile tanks would be needed for R.E. work until we had Tank Field Companies working with tank battalions or brigades.

We therefore set out to design the necessary additions to a standard Mark V** tank which would enable us to use its power for a variety of engineering work. Some of this work was the special requirements of the Tank Corps. In addition to being able to lay a bridge across a canal lock under fire, these requirements included wire pulling with grapnels (described in Chapter IV), mine-sweeping, cable burying with a mole drainer towed behind a tank, demolition work under fire; the Tank Corps had carried out some of this work during the war by detaching special crews from Tank Battalions and giving them special training, but it was obviously better that one unit should carry out all this special work, and it was a normal duty of the Royal Engineers. We did not, however, intend to limit the use of this mechanical power to Tank Corps requirements only, and had in mind many additional ways in which we could speed up field engineering by its use.

This tank became known as the R.E. Tank, and

PASSAGE OF TANKS OVER OBSTACLES.   131

the attachments which we designed for it are shown in the photograph. The arrangement was a simple one; hinged on the front of the tank was a jib, and this could be raised or lowered by a hydraulic ram seen on top of the tank. This was worked by a Janney Pump driven off the engine. With this tank the work that could be carried out was as follows.

The canal lock bridge could be picked up and the tank could advance cross-country with it and lay it under fire in less than a minute, no man being exposed to fire.

A heavy roller in two pieces, weighing over one ton each, could be towed from the end of this jib and thus moved in front of the tank cross-country. It was found that these would explode contact mines, and the tank would thus act as a minesweeper. Mines containing up to 9 lbs. of high explosive were tried practically, and their detonation was not found to be unduly unpleasant for the crew of the tank, though the blast usually lifted the front part of the tank a few inches.

Arrangements had been made to mount the tubular girder bridge on a pair of idle tracks, and it was found that by means of this jib the whole bridge could be pushed cross-country on these tracks on fairly level ground though the total weight was about 60 tons. On reaching a river the tank would go on pushing till the tracks fell over the near bank and the front end of the bridge hit the far bank. The bridge was then ready to take tanks, and it was found that under suitable conditions the bridge could be pushed across a gap up to 70 ft. in about one minute from the time of arrival at the gap. No man was exposed to fire during the process, the tank simply backing away to release itself from the attachment to the bridge.

The above work was mainly to fill the requirements of the Tank Corps, and other work for this Corps, such as wire pulling with grapnels, was to be carried out by these tanks, but in addition there was much general work on field engineering for which this tank could be used. The jib could lift a load of 10 tons through 12 feet in two minutes, or loads up to 15 tons could be raised more slowly so as not to overload the pump. This power of using the tank as a very powerful mechanical elephant was in constant use for moving heavy weights, transporting girders, etc. Trench cutting with a Fowler Plough was also tried, and it was found that a wavy trench could be ploughed which was about 3 feet wide at the top and 2 feet wide at the bottom and 3 feet deep. This was done in two cuts, and in each case the tank towing the plough travelled at about 2 miles an hour. This would have saved a great deal of labour if it had been available in France for the construction of communication trenches in back areas.

Another trial which we carried out was in connection with cable burying. A mole draining plough was obtained and towed behind a tank. This plough consists of a thin blade which is lowered about 2 or 3 feet into the ground, and along the lower edge there is a cigar-shaped bulb. A thin

THE "R.E. TANK."
The "R.E. Tank" carrying a bridge which it could lay under fire in less than a minute, across gaps up to 20 feet.

THE "R.E. TANK."
The "R.E. Tank" being used as a "mine-sweeper," with heavy steel rollers to explode the mines before the tank passes over them.

tube leads down to this bulb, and as the plough is dragged through the ground, signal cables are fed down this tube and laid in the tunnel left behind. As the plough passes on, the thin slot left by the blade closes up, leaving hardly any mark on the ground, and as many as 20 or 30 cables can be buried, if desired, in the small tunnel that has been made about 2 feet 6 inches under ground. The trials worked well, and no difficulty was experienced unless attempts were made to cross a beaten track or very hard soil.

Our official work had been limited to completing the trials with the tubular girder bridge and the canal lock bridge, but we soon extended the scope of our work far beyond these trials. Although it had been very successful in many ways, there were certain objections to the Inglis Tubular Girder Bridge. It was very expensive, and the same type of bridge had to be erected over short or long spans, although in the former case the bridge might be unnecessarily strong and heavy. We therefore investigated the question of an entirely new method of bridge construction, with the idea of increasing the speed at which we could build bridges for tanks. We designed a skeleton steel box which was about 4 feet high, 2 feet 4 inches wide, and 8 feet long. The box had eyes at each corner and at each end, as shown in the figure, so that other similar boxes could be fastened on by pin joints. In this way a long girder could be built up to any required length in 8 feet sections. The box weighed $12\frac{1}{2}$ cwt., so that it could be conveniently handled. To build a bridge, two, three or four girders could be used, and these were launched alongside each other across the gap. When four girders were used there was a space of only a few inches between them. With two girders in use

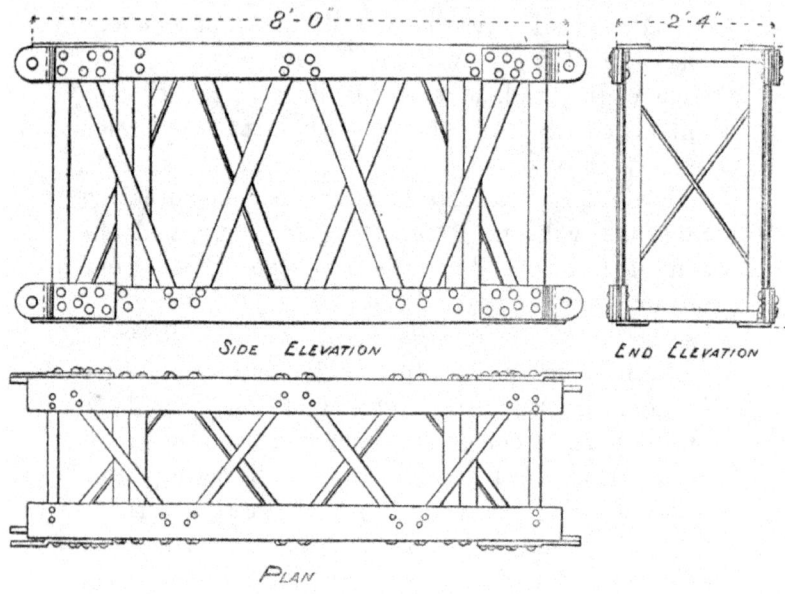

STANDARD BOX GIRDER

they were spaced 5 feet 6 inches apart; and with three girders the third was placed centrally between the two outer girders. The number of girders to be used depended on the weight to be carried and the span. For instance, 4 girders were needed to take our heavy tanks over an 80 feet span, but three girders were sufficient for spans up

PASSAGE OF TANKS OVER OBSTACLES. 135

to 48 feet. The girders had horn beams, i.e. ramped ends, to sit on the bridge seats at each end, and when the necessary number of girders had been launched across, timber decking was laid on top and the bridge was ready for use. There were thus only two essential parts in the bridge—the boxes and the timber deck planks, and there was not one bolt in the bridge. This made for extreme simplicity and rapidity in launching; it was never necessary to send up a heavy bridge of greater strength and weight than was needed for the shorter spans, because fewer girders could be used in this case; this made for economy in manufacture and transport. In addition, the bridge could easily be widened to take two-way traffic by adding more girders on one or both sides and increasing the timber decking. These points solved all the main objections to the girder bridges used in the war in an almost absurdly simple manner. The bridge became known as the Box Girder Bridge, and is now the standard girder bridge for the army.

During this time, about 1919-20, we initiated the work on the steel bridging trestle and the decked-in pontoon, and started considering equipment for the infantry assault bridge, all of which became the standard equipment of the army later, and also the anti-tank mine. The latter we thought should be quite a light, simple, contact mine. After a series of experiments we found that 4 lbs. of high explosive would cut the track of any tank that we would be likely to meet, and so stop the tank and render it an easy target for the artillery. We suggested a wooden box lined internally with sheet metal and provided with a contact fuse on top. For important depôts or bases in rear, no doubt electrical or other types of anti-tank mine would be required which could be made safe at will, but for forward area work in war the small contact mine appeared to be what was required. At the end of 1920 I left the experimental establishment at Christchurch.

In 1921 the heavy tanks which were still in use in the army were rapidly wearing out, and it became clear that no tank of this nature would form part of the equipment of the post-war army. It was far too expensive and immobile. It was, therefore, no use continuing with experiments to ascertain the ways in which tanks of this type could help us to solve the field engineering requirements of the Tank Corps, or the army as a whole. As we have already seen, the Vickers Tank was produced a little later, and also the Dragon for the artillery. The question of re-designing the bridging tank to carry a suitable bridge for short spans was then reconsidered. The problem, however, had changed. With the heavy war tanks we had a machine weighing over 30 tons and more than 30 feet long, and the canal lock bridge spanned 20 feet. We now had the Vickers Tank of about one-third of this weight and length, but we still wanted the same length of bridge, because nothing much less than a 20-foot bridge is worth carrying at all. This made the problem of design very difficult. After much trouble and thought a very clever design was prepared by Major H. H. Bateman, at Christchurch, by which a 30-foot bridge was carried horizontally on top of a Dragon. A Dragon was chosen because it was available at the time and the chassis was practically the same as the early Vickers Tanks. The bridge was launched by first pushing out light launching ways across the gap on which the bridge then rolled out. But even if the bridge had been fitted on a tank, it could not have been done under fire, as several men had to work outside the tank.

It would, of course, have been possible to build a special and very expensive machine by means of which a bridge for gaps of this nature could be carried up and laid under fire. We could, however, only afford to build a small number of such machines in peace, and they would be very vulnerable to fire from modern anti-tank weapons. Moreover, with the increased mobility at which we were aiming it was hoped that trench warfare conditions would be avoided and that this mobility could often be used to pass tanks across obstacles at a flank where the enemy's fire could be avoided. It was therefore decided to take no further steps, for the time being, to produce a bridging machine of this nature, but to concentrate on the development of bridges that could be constructed very rapidly.

During these years—1920-1926—the steel trestle and the pontoon equipment with the decked-in pontoon, and also the infantry assault bridge, were developed. Though there is some doubt as to the desirability of using wood for a pontoon that is likely to be required in the East, this work of development has produced an excellent bridging equipment. The work was carried out by the R.E. Board, with Major A. V. T. Wakely, and later Major H. H. Bateman, in charge of the experimental establishment at Christchurch. The anti-tank mine was also produced, though this has now been made stronger and heavier than our original proposals. No new ideas of any importance, however, had been made, and no new developments had taken place as regards the problem of passing fighting vehicles across obstacles.

Early in 1926 it was decided that a completely mechanized force should be formed for trials on Salisbury Plain in 1927. In the summer of 1926 instructions were issued that the 17th Field Company R.E. was to be mechanized to take part in these trials. I had originally thought that a force of this nature would move entirely behind armour protection, so as to be able to ignore the delaying action of the enemy using odd machine-guns to prevent us from moving round him. In that case the sappers would require light tanks or armoured cross-country lorries, so as to be able to accompany the force and carry out bridging and demolition work, as required. This had been our proposal at Christchurch just after the war. It was, however, decided that, at any rate to start with, there would be unarmoured troops as well as armoured in the force. In point of fact, the provision of either

The "Tool Lorry" of a Mechanized Field Company, R.E.

PASSAGE OF TANKS OVER OBSTACLES. 139

tanks or armoured cross-country lorries to carry personnel presents serious difficulties, both from a financial and manufacturing point of view. The other unarmoured troops in the force were to have half-track lorries; but the six-wheel lorry had just made its appearance, and the 17th Company asked for and obtained Morris six-wheeled lorries for the equipment of the company, and we never regretted the choice.

From the point of view of the passage of tanks over obstacles, the 17th Company had two main problems to solve. First of all, the leading troops in the mechanized force were to consist mainly of the small fighting vehicles which were described in Chapter XI, and it was essential that a means should be devised to pass them very rapidly over any water obstacles. These machines weighed up to 3 tons, and as a solution the company devised a raft made from the Kapok floats used for infantry assault bridges. Twenty-eight of these floats were to be used to form one raft, and the Kapok material is such that the raft remains buoyant for many hours even if penetrated by machine-gun bullets. The difficulty, however, was this. To have sufficient stability to take machines of this type the minimum dimensions for the raft were about 12 feet long and 13 feet wide. In order to avoid delay and having to carry out any constructional work in the water, it was desired that the raft should travel in one piece, so that it could be placed straight into the water and be ready for use almost at once. The dimensions of 12 feet by 13 feet were, however, too large to pack on a lorry which had to be able to pass other vehicles on a road. The 17th Company, therefore, devised a folding raft. It travelled upside down on the lorry, with the floats folded in, and in this position it could pass other traffic on the road; then, when it was required for use, the lorry could draw up near the river, but behind cover, and " open out." In this position the raft was 13 feet wide and sitting upside down on the lorry. The lorry would then dash down to the river, back round on to the bank, and the raft would be tipped over backwards into the water and be ready for use. In this way the Company would pass the small fighting vehicles rapidly over a river by using rafts of this nature, and they could count on having every chance of surprising the enemy and forming a bridgehead beyond the river by this means.

Having formed a bridgehead, the next step was to construct a bridge as rapidly as possible to take the whole of the mechanized force. For this, the normal army pontoon equipment was eminently suited, but so far no decision had been made as to its method of transport. This problem was given to the 17th Company to solve, and they produced two solutions. One was to use 3-ton six-wheel lorries, with each lorry carrying one pontoon and towing a trailer with the second pontoon, and carrying one bay of superstructure. The other was to use 30-cwt. six-wheel lorries fitted with Carriemore trailers, and carrying one pontoon and half a bay of superstructure per lorry. Both methods

The Modern Form of Pontoon Transport.

One floating pier and one 21-foot bay for loads up to 9 tons are carried on this lorry and trailer.

worked well, and both would probably be required on mobilisation for war. The Company were given four 3-ton lorries and one 30-cwt. lorry with Carriemore trailer, so that they were equipped with sufficient pontoon equipment for bridging the small rivers round Salisbury Plain.

There would, however, obviously be occasions when it was very desirable to be able to pass medium tanks rapidly over small streams. Although these tanks can pass through fairly deep water in fords, they cannot usually drop down the banks of a river and climb out again if the water is more than 2 feet 6 inches, or 3 feet deep at the most, and in any European country there are very large numbers of streams which are four or five feet deep and would form tank obstacles. To enable tanks to cross an obstacle of this nature the 17th Company devised some timber "stepping stones." They took the form of a skeleton timber box or crate, about 12 feet long, 5 feet wide, and 5 feet deep. These boxes could be packed up into a handy form for transport, and when required they were put together behind cover near the river and tied on to ropes which kept them about 4 feet apart. When everything was ready the sappers carried these forward and threw them into the river and picketed the ends of the ropes. These timber stepping-stones would then be floating on the water. Tanks could then approach and pass freely over them, pressing each down in turn to the bottom of the river. This method was used on many occasions, and tanks passed over streams up to 5 feet deep without difficulty. In November, 1927, the Company gave a bridging demonstration to the Dominion Premiers at Camberley, and showed them various methods of passing fighting vehicles over river obstacles. Among these they demonstrated the stepping-stones in use over a river 50 feet wide and about 5 feet deep. From the time that the sappers arrived at the river bank carrying the first stepping-stone to the time when everything was ready and the first tank had passed across was just under 60 seconds. It was, of course, a rehearsed performance, but it showed how rapid this method could be.

Another trial which they carried out was with what they called a " Mat " bridge. Timber panels were taken and joined together, edge to edge, and pushed out over the water till they spanned across the river. In this way a fairly rigid " mat " of timber was laid across the water. This mat had little buoyancy, but a considerable weight was needed to force it rapidly down through the water. Hence loaded lorries could pass over without sinking, because they were always climbing on to a part of the mat that had not yet begun to sink. It was found that 30-cwt. lorries could pass over, one at a time, at about 10 miles an hour. This work was carried out because it was thought that there might be occasions when it was essential to be able to pass a few lorries across at some place where it was not desired to construct a complete bridge, using up a large quantity of pontoon equipment. This type of bridge was not, however,

A Pontoon Bridge constructed in 40 minutes from the time of arrival of the first lorry carrying the equipment. The bridge will carry tanks up to 16 tons weight. A 12-ton tank is seen crossing over the bridge.

PASSAGE OF TANKS OVER OBSTACLES. 143

used in any of our manœuvres, and as it turned out in the end to be rather heavy, it would probably not be worth carrying as equipment.

In addition to the above work, the 17th Field Company aimed from the start at replacing man power by machinery for as much of their work as possible, thus reviving the work which had been started in this direction at Christchurch just after the war. This process is difficult to achieve in a field unit without lumbering it up with many different types of machines, but certain steps were found possible. In each section the lorry which carried the tools was fitted with a small jib and a winch driven off the lorry engine. This was most useful for lifting heavy weights, clearing obstructions in roads, and for bridging. An air compressor plant was another necessity, and after some difficulty the Company obtained permission to experiment in this direction and obtained the necessary plant. An air compressor mounted on a trailer fitted with pneumatic tyres was tried, and proved a great success. For demolishing bridges, the compressor plant enabled the sappers to cut into masonry arches and abutments and thus save much time and explosive when placing the charges, and in many other ways this plant was most useful. The Company also mounted a 20 ft. folding derrick on a 3-ton six-wheel lorry, fitted with a 5-ton power winch, and this was found most useful on many occasions for Field Engineering work.

Reference has already been made to the fact

that it had been decided not to pursue the construction of a special bridging machine for laying bridges under fire, but we were still faced with the necessity for evolving a rapid method of spanning gaps up to, say, 60 feet to take fighting vehicles. On investigation it was found that if civilian bridges are hastily demolished in war the clear gaps left by the demolition are less than 60 feet, in the majority of cases. The 17th Company therefore set out to see what type of bridge they could evolve to bridge gaps up to this span as rapidly as possible. The original box girder had been designed when we still had 35-ton tanks in the Service, and was necessarily heavy and slow in launching; but the heaviest tanks that we were likely to use in the field army did not now exceed 16 tons in weight. Moreover, the whole army, with the exception of these medium tanks and heavy artillery required for siege work, could pass over a bridge designed to carry 8- or 9-ton loads. The system of using box girders had proved so satisfactory for military purposes that it was obviously the type of bridge to aim at; but a much lighter girder would suffice for these reduced loads. The Company now set about discovering how to launch a lighter girder of this nature as rapidly as possible. After many trials they devised a very simple method. A launching nose 27 feet long was fastened on to each end of the 60-feet girder, which was then pushed out on rollers by hand. At the point when the girder was about to tip over, the launching nose had already reached the far bank, and 12 men could

A tank passing over "stepping stones," which can be placed in a river in a few minutes to provide a crossing place. The tank in this photograph is an early type of "close-support" tank, carrying an 18-pdr. gun.

double across to lift on the nose and assist in completing the launching process.

The first model of this new type of light box girder bridge was then designed. The detail design was carried out, to the 17th Field Company proposals, by Capt. R. D. Davies, under the R.E. Board. Each girder consisted of four box sections, each box being 16 feet long and joined together with pin joints. The end sections were constructed as ramps to lead on and off the bridge. Thus a girder could be built in 32, 48 or 64 feet lengths. With two girders in use the bridge would take 8-ton loads, and four girders would carry 16 tons. These were just the loads that were required, and a clear span of 60 feet could be bridged. For transport, one girder complete travelled on one 3-ton lorry, and the timber superstructure for the decking also travelled on one of these lorries. Thus three lorries would carry a two-girder bridge complete, and five lorries would take a four-girder bridge. The packing and transport and erection of the bridge was thus made very simple, and in their first trial over a 60-feet gap the Company erected the complete bridge with two girders and decking in just under 20 minutes from the time of arrival of the lorries at the site to the time when the first vehicle passed over the bridge. This was far ahead of anything that had yet been achieved in military bridging, and there is no doubt that the possibility of repairing demolished bridges by this method, in so short a time, will be a great asset from the point of view of mechanical warfare.

This light box-girder bridge is still being improved in detail by the R.E. Board, and its final form is not yet settled, but it should become one of our most useful pieces of equipment for military bridging.

All the above work was carried out on Salisbury Plain in 1927 and 1928, and the position in so far as the passage of tanks over obstacles is concerned, remains much the same to-day. Experiments are in hand to produce a handier rafting equipment than our improvised Kapok raft, and the pontoon equipment is slightly improved. From the point of view of the requirements of mechanical warfare we are well ahead with our methods of bridging.

The light box-girder bridge, constructed in 20 minutes. The fastest and handiest bridging equipment yet produced.

CHAPTER XIII.

THE ARMOURED FORCE ON SALISBURY PLAIN.

REFERENCE has already been made to the fact that shortly after the arrival of Field-Marshal (then General) Sir George Milne as C.I.G.S., orders were issued for the formation of a Mechanized Force for trials on Salisbury Plain, in 1927. The general idea was that the whole force should travel in mechanical vehicles, and it was considered that it should be capable of covering 100 miles in 24 hours. It was realised that a large part of the force would necessarily be in unarmoured vehicles, but it was considered at first that the escort of the fighting vehicles would be sufficient protection on the move. It was obvious that many of the vehicles with which units were equipped would not be the most suitable for use in this force, but it was better to make a start, using existing machines, and learn some tactical lessons, than wait for improved vehicles.

The formation of the force was hampered by a shortage at that time of armoured car units in England, and also by the lack of numbers of the new small tanks, or tankettes, as they were then called. The force, as it came into being on May 1st, 1927, was composed as follows :—

Reconnaissance Group.

One Company (16) Tankettes.
Two Companies Armoured Cars.

Main Group.

One Battalion (48) Medium Tanks.
One Field Brigade R.A.
One Light Battery R.A.
One Machine-gun Battalion.
One Field Company R.E.
One Signal Company.

The force was organised in the above two groups. The reconnaissance group, which acted really as the advanced guard of the force, was formed from the 3rd Tank Battalion, and the group was commanded by Colonel F. A. Pile. It will be seen at once how very short they were in numbers of vehicles; the original intention was that they should have about three times as many, but the vehicles were not available to start with. The formation of this reconnaissance group was not a fixture; sometimes some machine-guns from the machine-gun battalion would be sent up to accompany it. The light battery often went with it; and at other times, if we were approaching a river, a section of the Field Company would be sent up with rafts to enable it to cross rapidly and form a bridgehead.

The force was commanded by Col.-Comdt. R. J. Collins, C.M.G., D.S.O., with a small staff who normally marched at the head of the main group; All the units in this group were, of course, mechanized. The Field Brigade had two batteries Dragon drawn, one drawn by half-track lorries, and the remaining battery had self-propelled guns, i.e. guns mounted on a Dragon and protected by a shield. The Light Battery started by being carried on lorries from which it could not fire, but later the guns were mounted on half-track lorries. The Machine-gun Battalion was on half-track lorries. The 17th Field Company R.E. was the unit chosen to carry out the engineering work, and I was sent to command it. Both the Field Company and Signals used Morris six-wheel lorries, and were the most mobile units in the force with the exception of the Armoured Cars.

It is not proposed to describe the various manœuvres and field days in which we took part; they had full Press publicity at the time, and have been described in several military journals. In particular, a very complete account of all this work was published from time to time by Capt. B. H. Liddell Hart. Not only did he do valuable work by giving publicity to this course of progress which the army was pursuing, but by his writings he helped to enthuse the army, and often assisted in guiding general thought and policy in the right direction.

In this book it is, therefore, only intended to give an account of what lay behind the idea of forming a force of this nature, what rôle it was ordered to carry out and test on manœuvres, and the results that eventually came to light. This work was carried out during the summers of 1927 and 1928. During the first year the vulnerability of such a large number of unarmoured lorries had cramped the movement of the force through country where cavalry machine-guns or an odd armoured car might lie in ambush for the main group. To search the ground and ascertain that it was clear of all small parties of the enemy meant reducing the speed of the force to about five miles an hour, which was the last thing that we wanted. In order to avoid this it was decided that a force of this nature would have to use armoured lorries, and though there were definite practical difficulties in producing such vehicles, it was assumed in 1928 that all unarmoured lorries had light armour protection, so that they were no longer very vulnerable to an odd machine-gun that might escape the notice of the leading troops. The force was re-named the Armoured Force for 1928.

The underlying idea in 1926 had been a hope that we should find some form of mechanized or armoured force with a fixed organisation like that of a division, and which was capable of carrying out several of the existing rôles of army formations, only much more rapidly and effectively. It was for this reason that the force was composed of all arms, and although it was never stated, there was an idea that this might lead us to the discovery of the ideal composition of a division of the future. The force was given three rôles to try out on manœuvres, and these were tried both in 1927 and 1928. They were as follows :—

(i) Strategical reconnaissance in place of Independent Cavalry.

(ii) Co-operation with Main Forces.

(iii) An independent operation lasting up to 48 hours.

As a result of our trials during the two years it became quite clear that a force of this nature with a fixed organisation was unsuitable for carrying out such a variety of rôles. For the first rôle, high mobility was essential. The armoured cars possessed the necessary mobility; the tankettes did not fall very far short, and it was reasonably certain that improvements to these vehicles could be effected which would make them into light tanks of a type eminently suitable for this work. But the main body of the force consisted essentially of the medium tank battalions, and these tanks had nothing like the necessary mobility. It will be remembered that the Mark I tank had thin armour, and was considerably lighter than Mark II. The former had shown at Aldershot and elsewhere that it was capable of a high degree of mobility, but the extra weight in the Mark II had made a great difference. This increase in armour protection was essential, and a new system of clutches on the half shafts was introduced to meet it, but the Mark II fell a long way short of the mobility that we required. It was found that the battalion could only average about 7 miles an hour on a day's run which was mostly on roads or tracks, with a little cross-country work as well. Moreover, the medium tank was a more powerful machine than was needed for strategical reconnaissance. It is usually necessary to fight for information, but this fighting does not include anything like attacking a main position, which is one of the main duties for which medium tanks are used. Further than this, the medium tank represents a great deal of fighting power concentrated in one machine, and for reconnaissance work it is dispersion that is required. It therefore became evident that although the reconnaissance, or light group, as it came to be called, could carry out strategical reconnaissance, most of the main group was superfluous for this work.

As regards the second rôle, namely, co-operating with main forces on the battle-field, there was no doubt that the armoured force could render great assistance, but plenty of difficulties arose when we came to carry it out in practice. The object was to keep the armoured force well back or to a flank, and then bring it in—usually on the enemy's flank —as a surprise, and at the same time that the enemy was being attacked by the main force, but the difficulty of timing the two attacks was considerable. Then the arrangements for covering fire for a hasty tank attack of this nature presented many difficulties. One of the main duties of the machine-gun battalion was to provide this covering fire, but it never once succeeded in getting the machine-guns out and a proper plan made for the covering fire in time for the tank attack. The artillery fire was limited to one field brigade, with any assistance that the light battery could give. They always came into action remarkably quickly, and were very effective, but one field brigade was not a very powerful artillery support for such an important attack, and enemy anti-tank guns might remain effective under this fire and cause heavy casualties to our tanks. Attempts were made to assist with artillery fire from the main force, but with a surprise attack coming in from a flank this raised obvious difficulties. Then again, some of the units which existed in the force were not needed for this work; for instance, the distance for reconnaissances might not be long enough to necessitate the use of armoured cars, and light tanks might be more suitable for this work. The field company might have little to do, and additional artillery might be essential.

The third rôle was a little ambiguous. An independent mission might mean pushing forward to seize and hold an important locality out ahead, or it might mean working round and cutting enemy communications. In the former case, a convoy of armoured fighting vehicles might be required to protect the advance of lorries carrying infantry and machine-guns. In the latter case it might be possible to attach a few lorries carrying sappers and explosives to a formation of light tanks or armoured cars, and take them round and guard them while the demolition work was carried out. There might be no possibility in either case of having to attack an enemy main position, and there would, therefore, be little necessity for medium tanks.

We therefore see that for neither the first nor the third of our rôles was a fixed organisation of this kind suitable, while it might not be the most suitable for the second rôle. It was mainly for this reason that the armoured force was disbanded at the end of 1928. What was required was brigades, or small formations of armoured fighting vehicles, the units composing them being similar in characteristics so that they could march and fight together. Then for any particular operation the necessary additional assistance in the form of artillery or infantry or engineers could be added in the right proportion and of the right type. It was this that led to the idea of armoured brigades and the production of the manual on armoured formations. This will be referred to in Chapter XV of this book.

Although there had been a change of mind as regards the type and formation of armoured force required, yet we learnt a very great deal from the trials on Salisbury Plain. All units in the force worked whole-heartedly under our commander, Col.-Comdt. R. J. Collins, and he himself worked harder than anyone. It was all new ground. We had to discover how to march, to protect ourselves, to obtain information, to deploy for battle, to arrange for covering fire, to cross obstacles, and in all this work there was no precedent to go by. Many of the lessons which we learnt would apply equally to-day when using formations consisting largely of armoured or mechanized units. This work has been discussed in journals and brought out in some of our manuals, but a brief summary of some of the main points may not be out of place.

Our first trials were, naturally, in connection with marches. Generally speaking, the movement of large bodies of vehicles proved far easier than had been anticipated. Although we usually marched to march tables, it was not always necessary. On one occasion we were commanded by a cavalry officer on an exercise, and, when we moved, every unit was merely told where to go to and left to do it as it pleased, and in spite of the very large number of vehicles concerned no trouble was experienced. The reason for this, of course, is the speed. If you come down a side road with a mechanical unit and find another unit passing along the road down which you wish to turn, it is only a matter of waiting a few minutes for that unit to pass, whereas with infantry long delays of this nature would occur and have serious results if the march was not closely controlled. It was really surprising how easily our mechanized units could tumble into place and get there with the minimum of staff work.

The speed of the force varied very greatly between different units, and also depended, to a large extent, on the size of each column. When it was possible to move in small columns on different roads, or at different times on the same road, a far higher average speed would be maintained than if the force was moving in one long column. The reason for this is that with small columns the vehicles can open out to a greater extent. If a unit is moving by itself it can move at a high speed, and if there are one or two vehicles which are not pulling well, they can be left to catch up later, and the remainder of the unit need not be delayed. But if the force is marching in a long column and each unit sheds a few vehicles because the pace is too fast, confusion begins to arise and roads get blocked, and it becomes necessary to move at the rate of the slower vehicles. The great lesson, therefore, is that mechanized formations should march dispersed as long as possible, and only concentrate for battle.

This, of course, is not always possible, and in point of fact we did a great deal of marching in one column and evolved various rules and signals for these marches. Under these conditions we found 50 miles a normal march for the main group, and at an average speed of 10 miles an hour, excluding long halts. A distance between vehicles of 40 yards was found very suitable. Short halts were for 15 minutes every two hours, but it was only the whole-track machines that needed these frequent short halts; in fact, they set the limit on our speed in all marches. We used the ordinary motoring signals and the usual military signals for " Halt," " Mount," " Dismount " and " Advance." In addition, we used the following signals :—

Prepare to Halt.—Arm extended and waved overhead from side to side.

Stop Engines.—Hand waved horizontally across body (wash-out signal).

Start Engines.—Small circular motion of the hand, as though turning a handle.

Road Blocked.—Arms held out horizontally right and left.

When driving by night without lights the same

signals were made with a torch in the right hand, but " Advance " and " Road Blocked " had to be changed, and were signalled by a succession of dots and several wide circles at full extent of the arm respectively. We thus had a simple system of signalling for day and night, and it worked well.

If a vehicle broke down it had to pull in to the side of the road, if possible, and signal the rest of the column on. If it unavoidably blocked the road, the " Road blocked " signal was at once sent back along the column, and the first company commander, or officer of equivalent rank, had to decide if the road could be cleared or the vehicle repaired in a short time. If this was not possible, then a reconnaissance for a track avoiding the block was at once carried out and the remainder of the column directed round it. It will be seen later that a bad block occurred during manœuvres, and was caused by a tank breaking down in a cutting in a narrow lane, which completely blocked the road.

The signal company was, of course, one of the most important units in the force. Most of the work was done by wireless, and the unit had various sets for different ranges. They travelled in six-wheel lorries, and a suitable set could be sent with a group or unit which was detached from the main group. The force commander normally travelled in a six-wheel lorry fitted with a large box body as an office. A wireless vehicle travelled behind him, and wireless messages were taken from this vehicle to the office, or vice versa, on the move by a despatch rider on a motor-cycle. At first it was found that there was some difficulty in taking an envelope with a message from the despatch rider on the move, and a rather amusing device was therefore introduced to assist in this way. An arm was hinged at the back of the office lorry which could be lowered so that it projected horizontally in rear when required. At the end of this arm was a receptacle like an inverted top-hat. When the despatch rider had a message for the office he would run behind the lorry and hoot. The arm would then be lowered and he would put the message into the hat, which would then be pulled up and the message taken into the office.

A point that was brought out very early in our training was the difficulty of preparing and sending orders out to units with sufficient speed. The direct result of this was that all unit commanders in the main group had to march with the force commander, and they travelled in the office lorry with him. As information came in from the light group out ahead, or from the air, the force commander could discuss it with his unit commanders. When a plan was evolved the unit commanders would rejoin their units and act accordingly. As further information came in and changes became necessary, additional instructions had to be sent out, but everything had to be done at very high speed. The force might be advancing towards the flank of an enemy division which was on the march. A delay of even five minutes might bring the force two miles nearer and within artillery range. It therefore became necessary on such occasions to send orders verbally by officers, and the old idea of the A.D.C. was thus revived. These A.D.C. officers could explain the force commander's instructions far better and more quickly than any written orders transmitted through signals, provided that they could get to their destination, and they usually succeeded in doing so on motor-cycles. As bridges and roads cannot be destroyed in peace time, the field company often had officers to spare, and it was these that the force commander generally used for this work.

It was, of course, only urgent tactical messages that were sent in this way. The bulk of the work was transmitted by the signal company, and mostly by wireless. The Tank Battalion was also linked up by wireless from battalion headquarters to companies and sections, and one company had wireless in every tank. The wireless worked well, and when the force was moving in two or three columns with the light group out ahead, they were usually all kept in touch with each other and with the air.

One of our most successful exercises during training was the last two days in the 1927 trials. Eastland, to which our mechanized force belonged, was at war with Westland, and a deadlock had ensued north of the River Thames. Westland sent one division (less one infantry brigade) and a cavalry brigade southwards to turn our left flank, and Eastland sent the mechanized force to counter this move.

The exercise commenced at 8 a.m. on the first

day. The Mechanized Force was at Micheldever, though the enemy believed it to be at Newbury (see map, page 164). The hostile cavalry brigade was believed to be about West Lavington, whereas it was actually at Heytesbury. The division was known to be in the Warminster area, and was actually at Heytesbury also.

The Mechanized Force had the use of one fighter squadron and one army co-operation squadron R.A.F., while the enemy had one bombing and one army co-operation squadron.

The O.C. Mechanized Force did not know on what line the enemy division would advance, but its rôle was obviously to advance eastwards, and he assumed that their cavalry would be able to secure the crossings over the Avon as far south as Amesbury, and that the division would march towards Tidworth. Actually, their advance was controlled by the director of the operations in order to ensure that the exercise would bring out the lessons he required, and the division was ordered to advance on the River Avon via Tilshead, leaving Heytesbury at 4 p.m. on the first day.

The commander of the Mechanized Force decided to move at full speed to the aerodrome at Old Sarum and to send the reconnaissance group on ahead to seize Avon Bridge and the bridges at Stapleford and Berwick over the River Till. He would then be in a position to strike northwards on to the flank of the enemy if he endeavoured to march eastwards. He would be able to attack on either side of the Rivers Avon or Till, and by attacking northwards he would be free from the cramping effect of having to cross rivers or tank obstacles while doing so.

The Mechanized Force moved according to plan. The reconnaissance group advanced at full speed, and the armoured cars reached the furthest bridges by 8.55 a.m.—a distance of about 30 miles. They moved with the combination of dash and judgment which they exhibited in all our trials. A little later these bridges were taken over by the Machine-gun Battalion, and the reconnaissance group was ordered to find and watch the enemy cavalry brigade.

The main group, with the tanks, reached the aerodrome at Old Sarum at noon. The O.C. Mechanized Force had asked for extra assistance from fighter squadrons of aeroplanes to drive away enemy machines, in the hope that his move to Old Sarum would be undetected; but this was not allowed, and the move was reported by enemy aeroplanes. One of the objects in moving to Old Sarum was that our aeroplanes could land there, so that all information brought in was readily available, and clear verbal instructions could be given to the pilots, and this proved of great value.

Actually, the tanks moved into an aeroplane hangar for concealment, but this was a mistake, because we had been seen and were bombed in a concentrated group.

No enemy movements were reported till 4.30 p.m., and nothing further had happened till then except some skirmishes between the reconnaissance group and enemy cavalry on the line Amesbury-Shrewton. At 4.30 p.m. the enemy were seen leaving Heytesbury and marching on Chitterne. The O.C. Mechanized Group at once ordered the main group to march to Yarnbury Castle, and the reconnaissance group with the machine-gun battalion were to hold off the cavalry and protect the right flank of the main group. Owing to an unfortunate block in a sunken road just north-west of Stapleford, the main group was not concentrated at Yarnbury Castle until 6.15 p.m.

By this time the enemy were advancing on Tilshead in a long column about four miles long, and with a screen or flank guard to protect their right flank, which was composed of most of his artillery. The O.C. Mechanized Force now decided to attack with two companies of tanks, supported by his field artillery brigade and assisted by the squadron of single-seater fighters. It was a most spectacular attack, and quite thrilling to watch. The fighters swooped down on the enemy guns just as the tanks were approaching, and would certainly have been most effective. The tanks charged through the gun line with every available weapon firing, and passed on to attack the infantry, on whom they inflicted very heavy casualties.

A little later, and just before dusk, the third company was sent through. Advancing in semi-darkness, this attack came as a complete surprise, and caused further heavy casualties to the infantry, who were forced to scatter in every direction.

The fact that the light was bad and that the O.C.

Mechanized Force succeeded in launching the fighter aeroplanes at the crucial moment saved the tanks from unduly heavy losses; but even then the umpires judged that 10 out of their 48 tanks were knocked out. Against this they estimated that practically a whole infantry brigade and the equivalent of two batteries of guns were out of action.

It was now dark, and the Mechanized Force moved into a laager for the night just west of Shrewton, while the umpires allowed the division to concentrate at Tilshead, where they were followed up and picqueted by the reconnaissance group. They continued their march to Crossing B at midnight, but unfortunately this information, which was sent in by the reconnaissance group, did not reach headquarters Mechanized Force till 2.30 a.m. on the following morning, owing to a despatch rider breaking down. The main group at once went off in pursuit and drove in the enemy rear guard, but the bulk of the division (or what would have been left of it in war) crossed the river, and the exercise came to an end.

Although the work of the Mechanized Force met with considerable success, and appeared to justify the use of a force of this nature for this purpose, it must be realized that it lost nearly 25 per cent. of the tanks in one encounter, and might have lost much more. A commander will grudgingly spare his expensive medium tanks unless he expects decisive results from which his main body can take advantage. In this case it is debatable whether a larger number of smaller tanks with greater

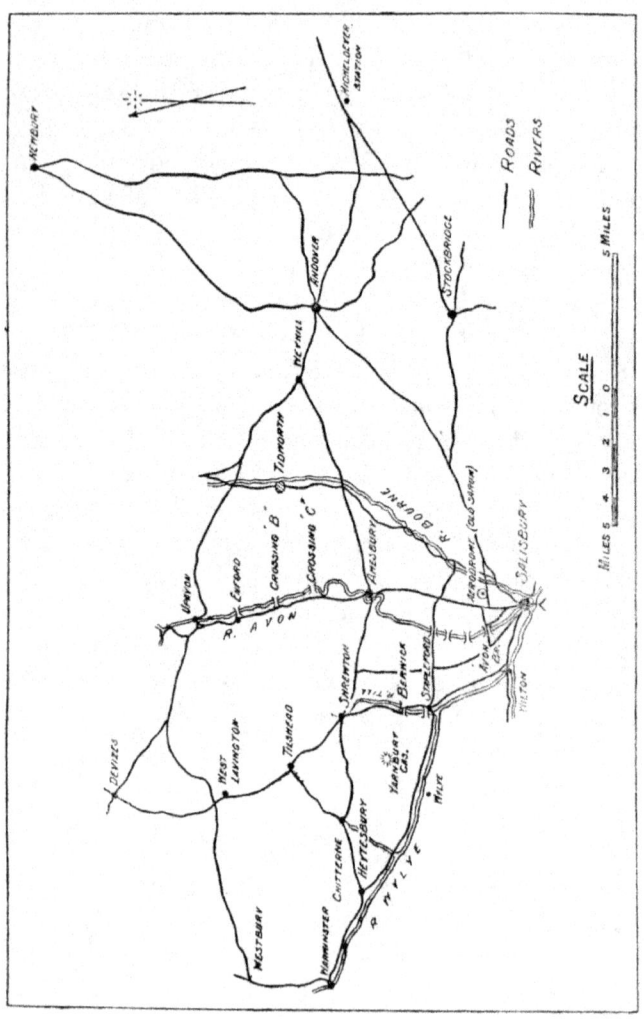

mobility could not have evaded the screen of guns and been as effective in this work with fewer casualties. The exercise brought out clearly what a great threat an armoured formation will always be to an advancing division, but the possibility of carrying this out at a smaller cost is discussed in Chapter XVI.

During the winter 1927-1928 we prepared a " battle drill " for various operations based on our past experience. The idea was a valuable one. Although many operations had to be treated separately, there were a large number, such as passing over an obstacle, moving into an area to lie up for the night, etc., for which we evolved a drill, and everyone knew what everyone else would do. This saved much time and confusion.

If within striking distance of the enemy, we moved into laagers when we halted for the night. The fighting vehicles were located round the perimeter and the remainder inside. To minimise casualties from bombing or long range artillery, if we were located, we usually distributed the force into three or four laagers, and vehicles had to be a minimum of 10 yards apart. Every vehicle carried a tarpaulin. This could be spread over it and helped to conceal the vehicle when lying up by day, or if under view from aeroplane flares by night, and also provided shelter for the crews.

Every unit had an illuminated sign to mark headquarters when lying up by night, and this had a hood to make it invisible from the air. By day unit headquarters were marked by a flag. The

M

headquarters vehicle in every unit was marked by a sign on the top right-hand side of the windscreen, and this was illuminated by night. These signs made it easy for despatch riders to find headquarters of units in bivouac, and also when passing the column on the march.

We practised the passage of obstacles on several occasions. In one case we crossed the River Avon just below Bulford. Light tanks were first rafted across to form a bridgehead, and a little later the pontoon vehicles were sent up for the construction of a heavy bridge to take the whole force. The river was over 80 feet wide at this point, and the bridge was completed ready for the first medium tank to pass across in 40 minutes after the arrival of the first lorry with bridging equipment. There was a slight accident after the first few tanks had passed over, but this was a minor technical fault and was soon rectified. Before this trial, it had not been thought that a bridge to take up to 16-ton loads could be constructed across a river of this size in anything like so short a time, especially as it included the off-loading of the equipment, weighing about 22 tons, from the lorries and trailers. A total of 80 sappers was used on the construction of the bridge.

On another occasion we tried forcing the passage of the Avon further north. The river was quite narrow at this point, but the exercise was set so that the river had to be crossed after a night march and without previous reconnaissance. The result was in the nature of a failure, and this has been mentioned by some writers, but the dice were so heavily loaded against us in this exercise that it was not a fair test, and such conditions would not normally have arisen in war.

Concealment from both the ground and the air was, of course, studied very carefully. After a number of trials a system of painting for all vehicles in the force was adopted. This consisted of a battleship grey colour for the top half and khaki for the lower half, the two being divided by a horizontal black line two inches wide. This gave a good effect both from the air and the ground under average conditions. Nothing really effective was found as a protection for vehicles in the open against the aeroplane camera. Deception was, however, carried out by making one type of vehicle look like something else. On one occasion eight lorries were dressed up very effectively like medium tanks, and completely deceived the air. When lying up by day under cover of trees, etc., we concealed the whole force from the air more than once, but great attention had to be paid to tracks left by vehicles or they would give away the whole position. All vehicles had to move under cover by the same track, an old existing track if possible. Tanks were not allowed to " swing " sharply when entering cover, as this left an unmistakable mark.

The question of supplying the force with the necessary petrol and oil and food was also studied during the winter 1927-1928 in an Administrative Exercise which was held. The idea had been that a force of this nature should be capable of being maintained at a distance of 100, or even 200, miles from railhead, but the exercise which we carried out showed that this was far from easy. The heavier lorries could not count on a radius of action of more than 50 miles in war, if they had to do it every day, and the system of handing over to a second convoy of lorries the supplies carried in the first, including enough petrol to fill up their tanks, soon becomes inefficient if carried into many stages. Moreover, all convoys might have to be protected by being accompanied by fighting vehicles, and meeting points where dumps were formed required protection. To maintain the force at a distance of 170 miles from railhead a train of 30-cwt. lorries in three echelons, numbering a total of about 300 lorries, would be needed, and in addition, a maintenance company totalling some 150 3-ton lorries. These were alarming figures for the maintenance of a comparatively small force. They showed quite clearly that for work such as strategical reconnaissance, where great mobility was required, the inclusion of such heavy vehicles as medium tanks and Dragons, with their very high patrol consumption and possible ammunition requirements made the administrative demands prohibitive.

A possible solution was for the force to go out for a limited number of days and cut itself adrift from communications for that period. In this case it worked out that if the force took with it 120 six-wheel 3-ton lorries it could travel 180 miles and have two average fights. The force would have to carry hard rations for, say, three days and return on the fourth. To help us in this direction the Royal Army Medical Corps investigated the question of producing suitable food in tabloid form, and claimed that the swallowing of one of their pills gave a suitable feeling of repletion for several hours. We never tasted these, but as we used to work almost all day and night during manœuvres, we asked if we might have a pill which would produce the feeling of having had a night's rest. This, however, was not forthcoming.

Most of the above trials and the lessons which they produced were initiated in 1927. Many were confirmed and more knowledge was gained under the direction of General Sir A. A. Montgomerie Massingberd, who controlled the work during 1928. The work was strenuous, but in spite of our labours the force was a happy family, and although we fully understood the reason and necessity for it, we all regretted the disbandment of the force at the end of 1928.

CHAPTER XIV.

ANTI-TANK DEFENCE.

It is a curious fact that although the British Army, and most foreign armies, have carried out a considerable amount of experimental work in connection with tanks, yet no one has developed the anti-tank side to any serious extent. The comparative failure of the Germans to do so has already been briefly referred to in Chapter III. They realised their mistake in the end, but even then they merely tried to produce large numbers of heavy machine-guns, which is only one portion of the whole problem of anti-tank defence.

If tanks play a very important part in a future war, then the anti-tank problem will have to be dealt with from the start, and not left till the tanks appear on the battle-field. Factories where they are constructed must be bombed from the air, woods where they might lie up in concealment behind the front should be gassed to prevent them from doing so, and offensive action must be taken against them from the start. The Germans failed completely in this direction. All our tanks and spare parts and reserves were concentrated in a comparatively small area round Bermicourt, near St. Pol, and great damage and disorganisation might have been effected by bombing just before an offensive, but we were left practically unmolested.

ANTI-TANK DEFENCE.   171

As enemy tanks approach the front, it becomes one of the most important tasks of our army co-operation squadrons to watch them so closely from the air that their every movement is known. This will entail night flying and observation with flares, and probably an increase in our present numbers of aeroplanes earmarked for army co-operation work.

To assist in this work various devices were tried by ourselves during the war in an endeavour to hear or detect the advance of tanks towards the enemy front line. Large sound trumpets were tried, and detectors to note ground vibrations were used experimentally to determine whether tanks were advancing during the night. The trials were continued after the war, but little success was achieved.

Having done everything that is possible in this way, the next step is to restrict the advance of enemy tanks. If a position is to be held, against which tanks are expected to attack, every use must be made of natural tank obstacles, such as steep banks, copses, etc. Even if these obstacles cannot stop the tanks, they may slow them down considerably and make them a far easier target for the anti-tank guns or artillery. Natural obstacles can often be improved into serious tank obstacles with very little work. Artificial obstacles can be constructed, but they take time and cannot usually be attempted in mobile warfare, except, perhaps, for short lengths to join up natural obstacles. Concrete stumps, like tree stumps, have been used for this purpose, but they require large quantities of material and labour and organisation. A simpler obstacle is a V trench with an almost vertical side facing the enemy, and the other side sloping at about 30 degrees towards him. This has to be six feet deep to stop a medium tank, but three or four feet will stop a light tank.

The best type of artificial obstacle is, of course, the mine. In a war where there are large numbers of tanks, and tank raids may be expected, it would seem that two types of anti-tank mine will be required. For guarding important depôts or railway centres in rear, a proper mine-field with electrically controlled mines will be needed. These could be fairly large mines, and their explosion would wreck the tank, and they could be rendered quite safe when desired by electrical means. For forward work, it would not normally be possible to transport and carry large mines, nor would there be time to install an electrical control system. The only chance would be to use small contact mines, which would contain sufficient explosive to break the track but not to wreck the tank. This would, however, definitely stop the tank, which could then be knocked out by artillery.

We have experimented chiefly with the latter type of mine, and although we have not reached finality in design, it is obvious that a small contact mine can be made which will not weigh more than 10 lbs. and will break the track of any tank which we are likely to meet. In order to be sure of stopping every tank, these contact mines could not

ANTI-TANK DEFENCE.

be spaced much further apart than about one foot from centre to centre. A considerable weight of mines would, therefore, be required to close a long length of front against tanks. For instance, a mile of front would require 24 tons of these contact mines. If the frontage normally occupied by a Division in defence is taken as about 7,000 yards, then a Division will need almost 100 tons of mines to protect the whole front. This seems a very large figure, but is not unreasonable when it is compared with the tonnage of ammunition expenditure.

Small mines such as these can, of course, be laid on the surface of the ground, and in grass or scrub they will be comparatively invisible. For that matter it does not make much difference if they are visible or not, because the enemy tanks could hardly pause during an attack to try and remove them or destroy them by fire before passing over them. Even if their exact position was known to the enemy artillery, it would require a prohibitive expenditure of ammunition to make gaps in a line of mines by artillery fire. The work of laying mines in this way can be carried out very rapidly, provided the transport is available to bring them up. Given about 30 three-ton six-wheel lorries, it is probable that a Division could protect its front in this way by a single line of mines in a very few hours and with very little labour.

If it is decided to bury the mines, then more labour and time is required; but even then, seven men working with each lorry will bury all the mines contained in that lorry in about two hours after arrival at the site.

Anti-tank mines are, therefore, a serious problem from the tank point of view, even in comparatively mobile operations. We have not, so far, started to tackle this problem seriously. As mines were becoming a serious problem before the end of the war, we had begun to tackle it, and produced the tank mine sweeper, with rollers in front, which was described in Chapter XII. Heavy rollers of this nature could, of course, only be manipulated by using the powerful war-time tanks, and when these were superseded by the modern medium tanks no further trials were carried on in mine sweeping.

One other proposal was made during the war as a means of enabling tanks to pass over a minefield. It may either interest or amuse the reader, but

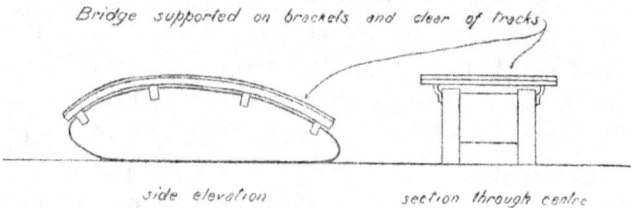

although it appears almost a comic suggestion, there is no reason why it should not work, and it would probably have been tried if the war had continued, and it would then possibly have been taken quite seriously. The proposal is self-explanatory from the diagram.

It will be seen that a special tank has been

devised which is lower in front than normal tanks, and a bridge is constructed over the top of the tank which is quite clear of the tank tracks. The idea was that the tank would only contain one or two men to drive the machine, and that they should be provided with an inner box with a secondary armour protection. The tank, or a number of such tanks, would advance to the attack just in front of the fighting tanks. On reaching the line of minefields the tanks would be stopped by the explosions, but would then remain in the gap and the fighting tanks could follow and climb over their backs and carry out the attack without themselves passing over the line of mines. This device would, of course, only have worked when dealing with one line of anti-tank mines, or when two or more lines were located quite close together, which is often done to produce a tank-proof belt without putting the mines so close together as one foot. A single line or belt is, however, as much as an enemy would often be able to construct, except in static warfare. The crew of this special tank would be quite safe from the explosions of the enemy contact mines, which, like ours, would probably only aim at breaking the track and stopping the tank.

Several other devices and schemes for stopping tanks and armoured cars have been suggested and tried at various times. For armoured cars a very effective and simple device is to stretch a thin steel wire between two trees or pickets across the road. The wire should cross the road on the slant, making an angle with the road of 30 or 40 degrees. The wire should be about 2 feet above the ground. The armoured car advancing at high speed will have difficulty in seeing the wire, and as the front wheel strikes the wire the steering will be taken out of the hands of the driver and the car will probably turn turtle in the ditch at the side of the road. Another and even simpler device for stopping armoured cars consists of using a plank about 2 inches thick, with a number of spikes projecting 3 or 4 inches above the plank. The spikes should be about 3 inches apart and should be barbed. The planks should each be about 8 feet long and should stretch across the road, and they should be under fire, so that the crew of the car cannot dismount and remove them. If the car tries to pass over the planks the action is as follows : the spikes penetrate the tyres and the barbs hold them there. As the car passes beyond the plank the latter rises up with the wheels, being held to the tyre by the spikes. The plank then usually hits the steering rod and disables the car; in any case, it is bound to do considerable damage to both the car and the tyres. Both these methods can be used on manœuvres so long as the Umpires are told and can warn the cars to move carefully, and when they are restricted in this way, the action of the armoured cars becomes much more realistic, and like actual war conditions, than is usually the case on manœuvres.

Both in thought and trial all the above work in connection with anti-tank defence is a long way behindhand compared with the progress that we have made with tanks and mechanical warfare; and when we come to the actual anti-tank weapons themselves we are equally far behind. Most nations have experimented with half-inch and larger sized machine-guns for anti-tank work, and with small size guns, but as the work has gone so slowly no one is at all certain yet whether a machine-gun or a light gun is the most suitable weapon, and much more experimental work and tactical trial will be needed before we can go to production and equip all units with their anti-tank weapons. The present proposal is that an infantry battalion will have four of these weapons when the type has been settled.

There is much diversity of opinion as regards its method of carriage. There are those who argue that as the weapon is too heavy to manhandle, it must have a mechanical means of transport, and as it must be able to move cross-country, it must be equipped with tracks. Further, that in order to have some protection from the small-arm fire of tanks, it must be armoured if it is to be able to take on tanks and knock them out. They then argue that this is practically a tank, and that the only answer to a tank is another tank.

There are, however, many good reasons for putting the argument in quite another way. Tanks are weapons of offence; they are also very expensive weapons, and it is very undesirable to have to keep a number of them on defensive parts of the front to meet enemy tank attacks. Then again, although tanks may be very effective for counter-attacking enemy tanks after they have penetrated our lines, it is obviously best to break down the enemy tank attack before it has reached our foremost troops. For this purpose concealed anti-tank weapons are required and not a rather large and conspicuous tank. An anti-tank defence that avenges the death of the infantrymen by destroying the tanks at a later stage, is not nearly so popular with them as weapons to stop the tanks before they deliver their attack.

Now a tank that has to fight, in and among the enemy, in comparatively small numbers needs all-round armour protection, all-round fire, and a fair length of track so that obstacles can be crossed. This means a fairly heavy machine, which means a powerful engine, and, consequently, an expensive tank. Hence any tank that can carry an anti-tank weapon must be expensive. For defensive purposes, however, we need nothing like this. We can have a small tractor which either tows or carries an anti-tank weapon. It does not need high speed, nor any great obstacle-crossing capacity, because the infantry can ease a way for it over bad obstacles; and the armour can be limited to a good shield for the gun and the firing numbers. This is a very different machine to a tank. It can be far cheaper, and therefore we can have more of them, and we can distribute them permanently to units which we could never afford to do with expensive tanks. The machine can be made much lower and more inconspicuous than a tank, and it is on these lines that we are now working.

ANTI-TANK DEFENCE. 179

A machine of this type can hide behind quite low cover and fire with the gun mounted; in this way it would remain mobile and could be rushed to a threatened flank, if necessary. Alternatively, the gun could be dismounted and used from the ground in more stabilised warfare. Such a machine might well be developed so that it can fire on the move and thus afford some protection to a column on the march if attacked by tanks.

An interesting type of anti-tank weapon was devised during the war and tried out, but never used in practice. It was an anti-tank rifle grenade. The charge consisted of about 1½ lbs. of high explosive in a thin case. The idea was that these grenades should be kept in the trenches as trench stores. On the approach of tanks the men would load their rifles with them, and as the tank passed over or near a trench the grenades would be fired straight at it from 20 or 30 yards distance. From this range the grenades travelled fairly horizontally, and it was quite easy to hit the tank, and the result of the explosion was to knock a large hole in it about a foot in diameter. This device could, of course, be met by using matting to protect the tank on the outside, or by some similar means, to keep the grenade from actual contact with the armour plate; in any case, the available range was so short that the idea was dropped after the war. It would, however, have given the infantryman some means of hurting a tank if the Germans had attacked us with large numbers.

CHAPTER XV.

THE MECHANICAL ENGINEER IN THE MODERN ARMY.

WE have already discussed in Chapter VI the organisation which we developed for the mechanical engineering side of the Tank Corps during the War.

This worked well, but after the war, when mechanization spread in some form or other to practically every branch of the Army, it was obvious that a Tank Corps mechanical organisation could not meet the requirements of the whole Army, and the repair work was taken over by the Engineers employed under the Royal Army Ordnance Corps. The whole organisation at that time was a thoroughly bad one. The design work was in the hands of the Director of Artillery, who, as we have already seen, was reduced to a small staff for this work, and few of them had any knowledge of mechanical engineering. This work was under the Master-General of the Ordnance at the War Office, but, strangely enough, the Ordnance Corps who carried out the repair work came under the Quartermaster-General. To complete the muddle, the Royal Army Service Corps had taken over the maintenance and repair of all wheeled mechanical transport during the war owing to the failure of the Ordnance Corps in this direction; and they now retained this work under the direction of the Quartermaster-General. We thus had this very important mechanical engineering work divided among three branches of the Army and under two members of the Army Council. At times the position became quite absurd. For instance, when the half-track lorry was introduced, the repair and provision of spare parts for the rear half of a lorry came under the Ordnance, as it was mounted on a track! but as the front part of the lorry travelled on wheels it came under the R.A.S.C.

It is not suggested that this absurd position should never have arisen, or could obviously have been put right at once. The post-war Army had innumerable problems of reorganisation to face, and this was only one of them. However, as soon as Field-Marshal (then General) Sir George Milne became Chief of the Imperial General Staff the problem was taken in hand, and in 1927 a reorganisation took place which put the mechanical engineering side of the Army on a far better footing. By 1928 the following position had been reached. The design and experimental work was controlled by the Director of Mechanization, Maj.-General S. C. Peck, under the Master-General of the Ordnance, assisted by the Mechanical Warfare Board, acting in an advisory capacity. This Board was a thoroughly representative body, including several eminent civilians, and the detail work was carried out by technical committees composed mainly of fully qualified engineers. All this was a great improvement on the old state of affairs. The

Ordnance, who had now come under the Master-General of the Ordnance, were responsible for all repair work. We thus had a simple and straightforward organisation, under one member of the Army Council. The sweep was not, however, quite a clean one. The R.A.S.C., who had carried out splendid work, which has already been described in this book, stood out for permission to carry out the whole of their repair work. This they were permitted to do. Whether it was sound to allow this exception, and whether the Army is so large that it can afford to run two repair organisations is difficult to say. There was a suggestion that the reason for this cleavage was the fact that in the last war the R.A.S.C. had to deal with very large numbers of different types of civilian lorry, and that as the Ordnance were not able to deal with this, they would not be able to do so in any future war. This argument can, of course, be refuted. The motor lorry industry of the country is no longer organised in large numbers of small concerns, and in any case great steps have been taken towards standardisation even between large firms. Moreover, large numbers of R.A.S.C. vehicles are identical with the types repaired by the Ordnance. It looked, therefore, like an unnecessary duplication to have this second R.A.S.C. repair organisation. If this is found to be the case later, some adjustment will, no doubt, be made.

The technical organisation in the Army is, of course, a vital factor in the progress of mechanization. Without a thoroughly efficient organisation, new types of machine are not developed, or can only develop slowly, and existing machines cannot go through that essential progress of eliminating faults which eventually produces the perfect machine. The repair organisation is also of equal importance. The whole position is now, of course, very greatly improved, but it would be idle to pretend that there are not still faults in the organisation, some of which will be difficult to eradicate.

Just as there are two classes of employment in the Army, namely, Regimental work and Staff work, so there is just the same difference in mechanical engineering between the actual mechanical work and the direction, control and organisation of the work. We require both types in the Army. The actual repair work is "Regimental" work, while the control of the design and testing of machines and the organisation of the various branches and experimental establishments belong to the "Staff" side of mechanical engineering. This latter is work of primary importance, and yet it is often supposed that a good sound officer with common sense could do the work perfectly well. That is like suggesting that an able business man would make a satisfactory Chief of the General Staff without any previous training or knowledge. It is even sometimes suggested that mechanical knowledge is a handicap to those officers who are handling the Staff side of this work, as it leads them to interfere in details. This is akin to saying that a Senior Staff Officer should know no detail of any regimental work for fear of his being tempted to interfere. The truth, of course, is that just as a Staff Officer in the Army cannot have too much knowledge of regimental work, so these officers who are handling the Staff side of the mechanical engineering work should have some ground work knowledge of the subject itself.

This is not so difficult to arrange as it may seem. Junior Officers in the Army to-day often have a fair knowledge of the elements of mechanical engineering. They learn some of this at the Royal Military Academy, Woolwich, and perhaps a little at Sandhurst. As the Army is becoming more mechanized it would seem reasonable to suggest that they might receive a much more thorough grounding in this subject, which can certainly be grouped under the present popular head of general education. No one would dream of seeing cadets emerge from these colleges without knowing anything about riding or horses; why, then, should they now join their units without any knowledge of machines, although some of these units may depend entirely on the efficient state of these machines for their mobility?

Given, then, that officers in the future may have some ground work knowledge of mechanical engineering, how shall they acquire instruction in the Staff work side of this subject? This is taught, among other subjects, at the Military College of Science at Woolwich. At present the work at this college is hampered by the fact that some officers join for this instruction with practically no ground work knowledge, whereas others start with a good all-round knowledge. This, of course, will be put right in time, as we grow up mechanically in the Army. The eventual hope of those who are interested in this very important subject is that all officers will receive ground work instruction at school or at Military Colleges. Then certain officers who will be carrying out the Staff work side will undergo a Staff Course in Mechanical Engineering, in the same way as Military Staff Officers graduate at Camberley or Quetta. When this desirable stage has been reached we shall have officers with a ground work knowledge of mechanical engineering and specially trained in the Staff side controlling the mechanical engineering work at the War Office.

It is often suggested that this represents a Utopia which we cannot reach, and that these officers would have so much to learn that they could not be combatant officers with a knowledge of the requirements of the Army. That they should have served regimentally and understand the Army is obvious if they are to be capable of carrying out this very important work under the M.G.O., but there is not the slightest reason why this should not be accompanied by a knowledge of the ground work of mechanical engineering and a course in the Staff work side of the subject. Army Officers spend years learning special subjects to pass the examination into the Staff College, and then undergo an intensive two-years' course. They then possess a great deal of special knowledge, but this does not divorce them from their regimental knowledge of the Army. In the same way the officers who are to carry out this Staff work on the technical side should have the necessary specialist knowledge as well as a general regimental knowledge of the Army. We have taken a great step in reorganising the technical side of the Army on the present basis under the M.G.O., but we shall not get full value from it until the officers carrying out the Staff work have this essential knowledge.

From a psychological point of view, the matter is very important. Many engineers, both civilian and military, must work under orders from this Staff; these engineers do not expect the Staff to know the details of their own particular work; this would obviously be impossible; but they do expect that the Technical Staff at the War Office will be able to " talk their language " and understand their difficulties. Without the knowledge that has been referred to above, these Staff Officers cannot do this, and cannot, therefore, be efficient, however able and full of common sense they may be. The same applies to civilian engineers who come from civilian firms to discuss questions with the Technical Staff at the War Office.

This important question is gradually being put right. There are already several Staff Officers carrying out this work who have a first-class knowledge of the engineering side, as well as having a good knowledge of the soldiering side. The move in this direction is not, however, going very fast.

There are still many people who think that all we require are some good common-sense soldiers under the M.G.O., who will transmit in detail the requirements of the General Staff to the engineers concerned.

There is nothing that will retard progress more than the provision of an ignorant middle man of this nature. If he is there to explain the requirements of the Army he is doing the work of the General Staff, and should be serving under them. We do not want two General Staffs at the War Office. If he is there to examine and control the work of the experts and inform the General Staff of the results, then he must have sufficient knowledge to do so. Without this knowledge he passes on the information in an ignorant manner which irritates the experts beyond bearing, and the information is usually as incomplete as any other second-hand information. The mechanical engineers are baited further still by the statement often made that they need a common-sense officer, without mechanical knowledge, put over them to keep them straight. In every walk of life it is difficult to find really sound men with well balanced views and common sense, but the mechanical engineers have produced just as many as anyone else. Did Sir William Morris or Mr. Ford need anyone to keep them straight? Yet they were mechanical engineers with a detailed knowledge, and there are plenty of other examples of this. The mechanical engineer does not want to try and dictate to the General Staff, but when he gets his orders from them through the Technical Staff at the War Office, he expects them to be in his own technical language, and he has a right to expect this.

If the Staff side dealing with this work has its difficulties, the repair side also has its troubles. The general policy laid down in the Army for repair work is quite clear, and no one can deny that it is perfectly sound. It is based on the policy which we initiated in the Tank Corps during the War and described in Chapter VI, but with this rather important difference. In the Tank Corps we had Workshop Officers in every unit, who lived with the unit just like Regimental Doctors or Veterinary Officers. They knew the officers and men, and could use considerable latitude in interpreting the rules laid down for repair work. The Ordnance Engineers, on the other hand, do not, as a rule, know the regimental officers very well. There are, of course, exceptions, but as a whole they lead their own life, and being non-combatant officers, they do not take much interest in the soldiering side. They like to do all the work in their Ordnance workshops, and are constantly calling machines in there, even for small repairs. Our policy in the Tank Corps in France was to do all possible work with the Tank Crews in the battalion lines. This work hardly ever needs machine tools; it is nearly always work with hand tools, and the more of this work that the Crews carry out the more efficient do they become in mechanical maintenance.

As an indication of the way in which the Ordnance Engineers are separated from the

Regimental Officers, one finds attempts made to lay down what a unit may and may not do with their own personnel. We would not have dreamt of laying down such an arbitrary division in the Tank Corps in France. The division should be left quite fluid. As a unit improves in mechanical knowledge it can carry out more work and gain still more knowledge. If this work is taking too much time and interfering with other military training, the Commanding Officer can always step in and send the work to the Ordnance. It is obvious that minor maintenance must be carried out by the unit, and that heavy overhauls, when the whole machine is stripped, must be done in Ordnance workshops, but there is no object in trying to define a limiting line between these, and there would be no necessity to do so if the Ordnance Engineers were more closely bound up with the combatant side of the army. It has been suggested that this hard and fast line is necessary because without it the amount of work required from Ordnance workshops would be constantly fluctuating. This surely would be a temporary difficulty and would soon pass; in any case, there are always bound to be rushes of work in these shops, especially with new types of machines, which usually develop new faults about the same time.

From the point of view of economy, there can be no question but that units should do as much repair work as possible. Even if some of the units are not very highly skilled, and make some mistakes, it is cheaper to use their labour than employ civilian mechanics in Ordnance workshops.

All these points will, of course, gradually be put right. The Ordnance Engineers have had an exceptionally difficult time with the rapid growth of mechanization, and in their technical work they have achieved great results. There have been many suggestions that they should have their own Corps, and many people have suggested that this should be under the R.E. Cap Badge. By this they would acquire new traditions, for it was the Corps of Royal Engineers that introduced telegraphs, light railways, mechanical transport, flying and tanks into the Army, and have been responsible for initiating practically every step in mechanical progress in the past. They would, however, have to remain a specialist branch of their own. The "all round" Sapper who can do a little of everything could not take on this very important work as a side line. The Ordnance are storekeepers, and that is why the suggestions have been made that the Ordnance engineers should have their own Corps or join another engineering Corps, but which Corps it is does not really matter.

There are, however, many arguments in favour of making them combatant officers, even though there are financial difficulties in this direction. In France the Tank Corps Workshop Officers often had to fight with their men to defend a derelict Tank in the forward area on which they were working. In schemes with armoured forces they have to be left in very exposed positions working on damaged tanks, and must be largely responsible for their own defence. If they were combatant officers they would probably come in much closer touch with regimental officers, which would be of the greatest value.

It is difficult to know how all these problems will pan out, but a possible view of the future might show a fine Corps of Mechanical Engineers with combatant officers. The necessary regimental knowledge would be gained by having one officer attached to every large mechanized unit. This would entail no increase in cost because he would replace the existing mechanical Adjutant in the unit, but he would be of far greater value to the unit. He would be given plenty of latitude, and could work in with the officers running the mechanical engineering shops and stores, in accordance with the Commanding Officer's wishes. The necessity for hard and fast dividing lines would disappear, and the proficiency of units in mechanical maintenance should progress enormously. The Corps would also have its own mobile repair units, which could take part in all manœuvres, and thus keep touch with the soldiering side. The dealings of this Corps with the Ordnance would present no difficulty. They would, of course, take over all the Ordnance workshops, but the Ordnance would remain the store holders for spare parts. The inspecting of guns and gun-carriages, etc., would continue just as at present, but the actual work required on these guns would be carried out in a special section in these shops.

An extension of this proposal would be that the best officers would be selected for a Staff Course at the Military College of Science at Woolwich, or elsewhere, and they would then form the technical staff for the Army on the mechanization side. We would then have the whole of the work under one cap badge, i.e. design, experiment, test and trial, production and repair, and the officers who carried out the work would be officers who had spent much of their time with the units who use the vehicles as their regimental mechanical engineer. All the difficulties of finding officers with a combination of regimental knowledge and mechanical engineering would be solved, and they would be in a position to discuss all questions quite freely and with full understanding with the General Staff.

As regards the General Staff, it should be our hope that they may also in the future possess some general knowledge of the main difficulties in the organisation and control of this work, and that a very brief course of instruction in this side may, perhaps, be included in the courses at the Camberley and Quetta Staff Colleges. The instruction should cover in outline such subjects as mass production, materials, maintenance and repairs, and particularly the process through which any invention has to pass from the original idea to the time when it is produced in large numbers for use in the Army.

Our policy in the Army is to be ahead of all other nations on the material side. Sometimes we have machines which are a long way ahead and are kept secret. At other times it is the continued improvement of existing machines that takes us ahead of other armies. In either case, there are definite steps through which the munition or vehicle must pass on its way to perfection, and unless these are appreciated by the General Staff there is every likelihood of friction between them and the technical side. We shall not then get our new or improved machines at the earliest possible moment, and it is on this that success often depends in mechanical warfare. Let us, therefore, examine the stages through which a munition passes before it finally becomes equipment in the hands of the troops. These stages are :—

The stage of pure research.
The stage of applied research.
The design stage.
The production stage.

We will take these stages in turn and examine them in some detail.

Pure research is the seeking after knowledge without having any definite invention in mind. For instance, the discovery of Hertzian waves was the result of pure research carried out by Professor Hertz, and this discovery led to the invention of wireless telegraphy; but Hertz had no idea of inventing a method of telegraphy when he carried out his work of research. As a rule, the work of pure research has little to do with the soldier; the work is much best left to the civilian bodies, such as the National Physical Laboratory. The result of their work is always available if it should have any Military application. In the case of inventions for war the General Staff must set the problem, and the inventor then seeks among the results of pure research to find something which may lead him to his invention. As far as pure research is concerned, therefore, our duty is to watch the results and see if they may lead to some invention which may have a military application.

Applied research is the development of a particular invention, but without making that invention conform to any specification. For instance, about 100 years ago the possibility of obtaining mechanical power by the use of some form of gas engine began to be realised. The possibilities were obvious. Light and economical engines were required for the propulsion of road vehicles and small boats, and engines which could be heavier and more bulky were required for stationary work. But at this stage it would have been quite premature to enter the design stage and endeavour to construct an engine to suit any one particular class of work. What was required was a period of applied research. No one had any idea at that time as to what sort of oil to use or the best way of producing the gas; nor had they any idea as to whether the mixture should be compressed or burnt at atmospheric pressure. The designers had no data, and applied research was, therefore, necessary. One of the earliest attempts was an engine which sucked in an explosive mixture at atmospheric pressure and the mixture was exploded half-way down the stroke. The experimental engine worked fairly well, and a company was formed to produce stationary engines working on this principle. We now know that the principle was entirely wrong; none of the obvious alternative methods had yet been tried (such as compressing the mixture); and it was altogether premature to enter the design stage. The company went bankrupt. This was a very good example of the danger of entering the design stage when insufficient knowledge has been obtained from applied research. After this failure the necessary research work was carried out. In 1862 the Otto cycle was suggested, and later some experimental work was carried out on these lines. By 1876 nearly all the various alternatives had been tried, and a great deal of knowledge had been obtained. It was now possible to enter the design stage with a fair chance of success. Various designs were prepared for car engines and stationary engines, etc., based on the knowledge provided by research work, and these designs were now successful. But the same process would have been reached far more rapidly if all the available energy and money had been spent on research in the first place.

There are several modern examples, both during and after the war, in which we tried to produce an entirely new type of tank or other munition in its final form without carrying out applied research to obtain preliminary knowledge. A gamble of this nature is excusable in war, though it is seldom successful; but in peace the gamble of missing out the applied research stage is also sometimes taken.

This almost invariably leads to disaster and is inexcusable.

When sufficient knowledge has been collected the design stage starts. The first step is for the General Staff to specify their requirements. This is a most difficult thing to do, and yet through lack of knowledge of the pitfalls that lie before them, many officers think that the preparation of a military specification is quite easy. The more that the General Staff understand about the difficulties of the mechanical engineer the better will be their specifications. The difficulty in this work is that nearly all requirements clash with each other; for instance, if a higher speed for a tank is specified, a corresponding increase in weight or engine and a reduction in armament or armour has to be faced. The first point is for the General Staff to lay down absolute essentials; i.e. it may be essential for the front and sides of a tank to be proof against armour-piercing bullets under all conditions. These essentials, however, can only cover a few points. Everything else is a matter of compromise. For these the General Staff must say the degree of importance which they attach to each detail in the specification. This work must be done in the closest liaison with the technical staff, and as the work of preparing the specification proceeds it is their duty to warn the General Staff of any dangers into which they are running from a constructional point of view. For instance, the machine may be getting far larger than they have in mind, or unduly complicated and difficult to repair. This close liaison is most important, and is now well established in the Army, but lack of it has resulted in much waste and disappointment in the past in design work.

When the specification has been completed the detail design is carried out, and the munition must then be constructed exactly as designed and thoroughly tested out, under conditions as nearly approximating war as possible. The first trials and tests are carried out in experimental establishments, and later field trials are carried out by the troops. During these trials faults are bound to come to light, which must be put right and the machines again tested before production starts. It is an axiom that any new munition which has been designed will produce certain troubles which will require to be put right. It may be that the article is not suitable in some detail for use by the troops, or it may show excessive wear on some part, or an unexpected stress on some portion of a mechanism, but it is a practical certainty that a new design will require at least minor alterations as a result of trials. Just as a child has to go through measles and chicken-pox, and other minor ailments, before reaching manhood, so a machine usually has many minor troubles before reaching a stage where it is fit for production. The importance of allowing plenty of time for trials cannot be over-stressed. The cases where great delay has eventually occurred owing to undue haste in these trials are too numerous to mention. If production has been started and some trouble then arises during a trial, the difficulties of curing the trouble may be very great. The engineering industry of this country still laments the great loss in output of munitions during the Great War occasioned by lack of thoroughness during the design stage. Even a minor alteration in design must be most thoroughly tested before instructions are given for this change to be incorporated in the next order for production machines.

Lastly, when every detail has been tried and tested, the munition of war goes into production. Only for strong military reasons should any alteration be made to the design after production has started; the most important point as regards production is that every part of the munition can, as far as possible, be made by "mass production." Semi-skilled labour means mass production or nothing. Before the war the difficulty of production was never considered.

A munition, such as a gun, was altered and altered so as to produce the best possible gun without a thought being given to production on a large scale in war. During peace time there is plenty of skilled labour, and it does not matter how complicated the parts of a gun may be; there will always be sufficient skilled labour to produce the small demands of peace conditions. The result is that during peace time munitions tend to become unsuitable for mass production. This is a great danger, for it means re-designing many parts on the outbreak of a great war. In 1914 the engineering industry was aghast at some of the things which they were asked to manufacture. "Why make them like this?" was their cry. And the answer was that they had " grown " like that as a result of numerous alterations to try and get a perfect weapon. Even if the weapon is not quite so perfect, it is better to have a weapon which can at once be made by mass production than a weapon in which many parts have to be re-designed for mass production in the event of a Great War. Even to-day, though it is only 12 years since the end of the war, complicated parts are beginning to creep into our munitions; there are pieces of steel which are " cut out like cheese " in some weapons. This does not matter at present, for we are only likely to be engaged in small wars, where mass production does not arise; but these points should be closely watched in future.

All these points are, of course, well known to technical officers, and if this and similar knowledge could be extended to the General Staff it would save much misunderstanding in peace and war. They would only need the basis of this knowledge.

The necessity for the engineering knowledge has been laboured in this chapter, and purposely so because it seems as though we are only growing up slowly in this direction. Perhaps it is only impatience. Certain it is that unless we have the best possible technical organisation we will never fulfil our object of leading the world in this direction of producing small efficient Armies which can achieve their results quickly.

Exactly how this organisation will eventually take shape is hard to say; our present organisation is certainly sound in principle, and the views expressed in this chapter are only intended as suggestions or speculations as to how further progress can be made.

CHAPTER XVI.

PRESENT-DAY PROGRESS WITH TANKS.

IN this and the next chapter of the book it is proposed to review present-day thought and progress in the design and employment of mechanical vehicles.

These vehicles are now divided into three main groups. The first contains the Armoured Fighting Vehicles, which are designed to fight in and among the enemy, such as tanks and armoured cars.

The second contains the armoured carriers. These are vehicles which have some degree of armoured protection, so that they can approach close to the front and carry up weapons which are needed near the fighting line. Examples of this class are small armoured vehicles which carry a mortar or smoke-producing device to assist the advance of infantry, but are not required to move ahead of the infantry and advance in and among the enemy. Armoured anti-aircraft machine-guns mounted on lorries are another example. The armoured machine-gun carrier belongs to this class, though some of these vehicles are being improved so that they can be used more like armoured fighting vehicles, and this work is described in Chapter XVII.

The third group contains all the unarmoured vehicles, such as cross-country lorries, artillery tractors, lorries towing pontoon trailers, etc. To what extent the army will eventually use armoured fighting vehicles and carriers is debatable, but that the transport of the army will become more and more mechanized by the use of these unarmoured vehicles is indisputable. This is a process which is happening in civil life every day, and the army must follow suit to a large extent, even if it does not want to do so, because the older types of animal transport are gradually disappearing. These unarmoured vehicles have all been described in Chapter X.

This chapter will deal with the progress that we have made as regards the first group, i.e. light, medium, heavy and close-support tanks, and also armoured cars; while the progress that has taken place with armoured carriers and the use of un-armoured vehicles will be described in the next chapter.

Before any aspect of mechanization can be discussed it is necessary to have a definite knowledge of the types of machines available and their capabilities. This statement must not be taken to mean that the Master-General of the Ordnance at the War Office produces machines and that the General Staff devise tactical employment to suit them. The process is the exact opposite to this. The General Staff lay down what they require as regards the performance and capabilities of machines, and work in very close touch with the technical branch to ensure that they are not demanding the impossible. The machines are

AN EXPERIMENTAL HEAVY TANK.

It has a very good fighting body, with four machine-guns and one 3-pdr. gun.

then produced with a specification as near to the demands of the General Staff as possible.

At the present time a great deal of very valuable experimental work is being carried out by the Directorate of Mechanization, and in course of time new machines built to the demands of the General Staff, with entirely new capabilities, will appear, and will necessarily alter the tactical aspect of mechanization. No details can be given of this work, as it is obviously of a very secret nature; but the general capabilities of existing fighting vehicles, and the types of machine which we are aiming at producing at present, have all been published in books or pamphlets which are neither secret nor confidential, and which are available to the press. The outline specification of each type of fighting vehicle will, therefore, be given, to show what we are aiming at attaining in the near future or have, in some cases, already achieved. When fighting vehicles are mentioned in the remainder of this chapter they refer to vehicles built to these specifications.

We will take tanks first and start with the Heavy Tank. There is no proposal to make any large number of these tanks in peace time. The necessity for this tank has already been referred to in Chapter IX. The work is entirely of an experimental nature, and is a wise precaution taken in time of peace so that we shall be ready with our plans in case a war of the first magnitude should descend on us due to our commitments under the Locarno Pact. Incidentally, we have obtained a considerable amount of general knowledge from the experimental work on a heavy tank, which has been of the greatest value to us in designing Medium Tanks. A heavy tank would not be required at all in the early stages of a war, but might be essential to the achievement of a rapid success if the war lingered on for six or nine months and trench warfare set in. If the experimental work has been completed in peace time the production model should appear in the battle within six or nine months of the order being placed with the makers, and would save at least a year compared to the time taken if the whole of the experimental work had to be carried out after the necessity for such a tank had arisen in war. A heavy tank must necessarily be long, to enable it to cross wide trenches and obstacles, and the armour must be as thick as possible so as to be able to withstand the projectiles of the lighter types of anti-tank weapons. As, however, a war of the first magnitude, involving trench warfare and heavy tanks is a very remote contingency, the matter will not be discussed further in this book, and no more details about the specification of heavy tanks need be considered.

The Medium Tank is in a very different position to the heavy tank, and is at present our main armoured fighting vehicle. One of the main points in the design of a Medium Tank is to produce the steadiest possible gun platform at speed across country. A tank, after rising over an obstacle, crashes down on the far side if travelling at any speed, and when proceeding over rough

The latest type of 16-ton medium tank knocking down a brick wall to demonstrate its power. The gun turret has been swung round to the rear to avoid risk of damage to the gun. One of the two machine-gun turrets can be seen just reaching the line of the wall. This photograph is published by kind permission of the *Daily Mirror*.

PRESENT-DAY PROGRESS WITH TANKS. 205

ground in this way it "buckets" very badly. If the bumps are small ones, up to, say, 6 inches in height, the springs of the track suspension can absorb the bumps, but much rougher country than this has often to be negotiated by Medium Tanks. Many proposals have been made for overcoming this difficulty, but they all introduce complications, and at present the only partial solution that has been found is to keep the tank fairly long. This means a considerable weight, with all the disadvantages that weight brings with it, such as heavy petrol consumption and heavy maintenance requirements.

As regards armour, the tank must obviously be proof against small-arm armour-piercing ammunition, which means a considerable weight of armour. We are, therefore, committed to a fairly long and heavy tank; it is, perhaps, even more essential than for the Heavy Tank that the Medium Tank shall be able to protect itself, as far as possible, against anti-tank weapons. This means a good fighting body with one small gun and several machine-guns and a conning-tower from which the Commander of the tank can control the driver and the gunners and fight his tank efficiently. The remaining points in the specification of this tank are a road speed of 20 miles an hour, a trench-crossing capacity of six feet, a circuit of action on the petrol carried of 100 miles on the road and a fording capacity through a stream over a good bottom with water up to three feet deep.

The Mark II Vickers Tank comes fairly near to

this specification, but fails in some respects, particularly in the provision of a suitable fighting body. The latest experimental models of medium tanks are a great improvement in this and many other ways, and generally fill our requirements, but any tank of this nature must also have certain definite limitations, which should be remembered.

First of all, a tank built to this specification and with this length cannot be expected to weigh much less than 16 tons, with our present knowledge of tank construction. This introduces certain bridging problems. These are not very serious, because, as we saw in Chapter XII, we shall probably be able to deal with them, but a more important aspect is the difficulty of the mechanical maintenance of a comparatively heavy vehicle intended to travel at high speed cross-country. At present this throws a great strain on the transmission in the tank, which suffers accordingly. This will, no doubt, be put right eventually by mechanical improvements, or possibly by using tracks with lateral flexibility, as described in Chapter VIII. The Mark I Medium Tank was highly mobile, but it fell a long way short of our remaining requirements. The Mark II came nearer to meeting these requirements, but lost mobility in doing so. The difficulties of making a medium tank to meet all our requirements and retain high mobility are, therefore, obvious, and we cannot expect to get this at once. The medium tank built to our present specification is not, therefore, the type of machine which can be sent off for a run of 100

The Latest Type of Experimental Light Tank.

This photograph is published by kind permission of the *Daily Mirror*.

PRESENT-DAY PROGRESS WITH TANKS. 207

miles, followed by some fighting and a long march on the next day. There is much mechanical maintenance to carry out—adjusting tracks and brake bands—and this work takes time and labour.

A further limitation with this type of Medium Tank is its cost and petrol consumption. Accurate figures are not available, and approximations in figures are often apt to be misleading, but for purposes of comparison with other types of fighting vehicle it can probably be taken that this type of medium tank will cost about £12,000. The petrol consumption cannot be expected to be less than one gallon per mile on roads, and this alone imposes a distinct limitation on the mobility of these tanks.

We now come to the Light Tank. This is entirely experimental at present, and the most promising results have already been obtained. No details can, of course, be given, but the specification at which we are aiming is in no way secret. In this case it is again desired to produce a steady gun platform, if possible, but a high degree of mobility is essential. In the Medium Tank mobility was sacrificed to armour and stability, but in the Light Tank the sacrificing must be in the other direction. The maximum speed is to be 30 miles an hour, with 150 miles as the circuit of action. Armour to be proof against armour-piercing bullets from the front, and as far as possible from the flanks or rear. The armament to be one machine-gun with all-round fire, and a second machine-gun may be added firing .5-inch armour piercing bullets. The tank to be capable of crossing ditches 4 feet wide and wading through water 2 feet deep. The crew to be two, or possibly three, men. In its lightest form this tank weighs about 2 tons and costs some £1,500, so that it is somewhere about one-eighth part of the medium tank in weight and cost, and, of course, far superior in mobility. By mobility is meant its power of being driven for long periods without rest. As a rule, if vehicles are moving long distances in an advance towards the enemy, a road or some form of cross-country track is available, and the light tank could travel at high speed as well as for long periods. For a short distance over ground covered with obstacles the medium tank would, of course, be much faster than the light tank, and if the obstacles are serious enough the light tank might not get there at all. The term mobility is used above to include the question of maintenance. The light tank only uses reasonable quantities of petrol, whereas the supply of fuel, oil and spare parts for medium tanks in the field, at present introduces considerable difficulties if they are sent out ahead over long distances.

Other types of light tank are being tried which are a little longer and heavier and more costly. They can cross worse obstacles and are a little steadier on the move and may mount the second machine-gun firing the .5-inch armour-piercing bullets, but they lose mobility accordingly. These small and highly mobile tanks can only accommodate two men, but other types which are considerably larger and heavier, have a crew of three men. Some of these may weigh as much as eight tons, and are really a cross between the light and medium tank, in size, weight, cost and performance. It is sometimes argued that tanks with less than three men are useless, because they could not be controlled. The idea is that one man has his whole attention occupied in driving, and can in any case only see in front of the tank. The gunner has a revolving turret and can see all round, but his whole attention should be paid to looking out for the enemy; hence a third man is needed who shall be watching all the time for signals from the Section Commander, who normally follows just in rear with his Section Commander's tank and controls his section by signals. If there were no great difficulties in including this third man there would, obviously, be great advantages in doing so, but as far as can be seen at present it means changing from the small, inconspicuous, inexpensive and highly mobile 3-ton 2-man tank, to a 3-man tank weighing and costing at least twice as much and far less mobile. It is not impossible to overcome this difficulty of control. A shrill exhaust whistle or electrical device can easily be added to the Section Commander's tank, by means of which he can attract the attention of his tanks. The gunners would then look round momentarily through the back or over the top of the turret and take the Section Commander's visual signal and act on it.

All these points and different ideas are being tried

out, and in due course we shall, no doubt, arrive at definite conclusions, but for the purpose of discussion it is necessary to make an assumption, and for the remainder of this book the light tank will be taken as being the one which we described first, i.e. the 2-man 3-ton tank, with all-round fire from one machine-gun, carrying 3,000 rounds of ammunition, and capable of crossing or circumventing most natural ditches or obstacles in normal country. The maximum speed to be 30 miles an hour, and the machine to be highly mobile, so that 150 miles can be traversed in a day on good going with the petrol carried in the tank, and without needing much mechanical maintenance.

There is now a new type of tank which must be described, and which is known as a close-support tank. The main enemy of the tank is the concealed anti-tank weapon. In trench warfare this can be subdued by a barrage of smoke and high explosive, which screens or protects the advance of the tank. This, however, is a lengthy process and cannot be depended on in mobile warfare. Just as the infantryman needs close support from artillery or smoke when advancing in mobile warfare against enemy machine-guns, so the tanks need support to assist them against anti-tank weapons. It is true that the medium tanks already carry a gun, and therefore have a close-support weapon with them, but they cannot fire smoke, and in any case the danger of the concealed anti-tank weapon is so great that every possible assistance is needed. Nothing is yet settled in detail, but the proposal is that a number of these close-support tanks shall accompany the tanks in the attack so as to be ready to drown an anti-tank weapon with high-explosive or smoke the moment that it is suspected or seen. The specification of the close-support tank is to be very similar to that of a Medium Tank, except that the armament is to be a gun, howitzer or mortar, and possibly a discharger tube for smoke bombs. About 100 rounds of high explosive or smoke shell to be carried and 30 smoke bombs. Suggestions have been made that a lighter type of close-support tank should be constructed for use with light tanks. If light tanks, having an armament of one machine-gun only, are used, they have no means of attacking or protecting themselves from a few medium tanks or an armoured anti-tank weapon. The objection to light tanks being accompanied on long-distance work by medium tanks, or the above type of close-support tank, is that neither of the latter may possess the necessary mobility. Hence it may be found desirable to have a second type of close-support tank, consisting of a light and highly mobile machine, equipped with only one 3-pounder gun, or similar weapon, behind a shield. This would not need to weigh much more that the light tank, and would have the same mobility compared with them as the Horse Artillery had to Cavalry. The effect of this may be described as follows :— The medium tank, though it has many advantages, is in the nature of a moving fort, containing both, machine-guns as assault weapons, and a light gun as close-support weapon. If we split up the medium tank into light tanks for the assault and the latter type of close-support tank to back them up, we may get greatly increased mobility and increased safety by the use of dispersion. Against that we lose obstacle-crossing power and the concentration of fairly accurate fire which we can get from the medium tank.

Mention has been made in the earlier chapters of swimming tanks, and the possibilities of making tanks water-tight so that they can float across rivers or water obstacles. This problem has been closely investigated, and, as far as is known at present, so much has to be sacrificed in armour or armament to enable a tank to float that it becomes definitely much less valuable as a fighting machine on land. No attempts have, therefore, been made to make our modern tanks capable of swimming, but the problem might arise again if a few tanks were constructed for special purposes, such as for landing against opposition from a ship in smooth water, or for forcing a passage over a river. Other than any tanks which might be built in small numbers for a special purpose, it is unlikely for the present that our normal fighting tanks will be made capable of floating and swimming across water obstacles.

The Armoured Car has not yet been mentioned, and although it is now fading in importance, it is still a valuable asset to our list of armoured fighting vehicles. The success of the 17th Armoured Car Battalion towards the end of the Great War has already been described at the end of Chapter III.

This success was mainly due to the fact that the Germans had not adopted any plan such as blocking cross-roads, which is now a normal proceeding when dealing with armoured cars. The cars had rubberine-filled tyres, so that they could face some degree of machine-gun fire. Actually they had very thin armour, so that the weight was reasonable and gave them a fair mobility. The Germans were bluffed into thinking that they had the same protection as our tanks. After the war the blocking of roads cramped the work of armoured cars on manœuvres, and in order to give them some degree of cross-country mobility, so as to be able to avoid these blocks, they were equipped with pneumatic tyres, and eventually the six-wheel armoured car was adopted. This is our present model, and it has a fine performance. Speeds up to 45 miles an hour on the road can be obtained, and a circuit of action of 150 miles. The car requires very little mechanical maintenance, and is very reliable. On roads or tracks the crew can travel long distances without much exhaustion. It can travel cross-country at reduced speeds, but only on good ground, and its powers of obstacle-crossing are very small. The car is armoured against armour-piercing bullets, and the usual armament is one machine-gun and one .5-inch machine-gun for attacking enemy armoured machines. The crew is three or four men, with about 2,500 rounds of ammunition.

The normal use for the armoured car is medium or long distance reconnaissance where it will have little fighting to carry out. For this work the normal pneumatic tyre may be found satisfactory; but it is a weak spot in the armoured car. The tyres can, however, be filled with various substances, and the effect of some of these is that the tyre can still be used, even if it has been penetrated many times by bursts of machine-gun fire. The filling has, however, the effect of reducing both the road speed of the car and its already low cross-country performances. Thus, if the armoured car is used for anything in the nature of serious fighting, it has to fill its tyres with one of these compounds, and its mobility is then reduced to a position where it may not be much greater than that of light tanks. It therefore seems likely that only a limited number of armoured cars may be required in the future for use in medium and long-distance reconnaissance, where a high road speed is required, and that the closer work, for which armoured cars are now often used on manœuvres, which entails more fighting, may be carried out by light tanks.

During the last few years experiments have been made to try and produce a machine which could travel on either wheels or tracks, at will. Messrs. Vickers, Ltd., produced a very neat design, by which the track ran between the wheels, and the latter could be raised off the ground to bring the track into action. The advantages of some scheme of this nature are, of course, obvious. A high road speed is obtained on the wheels without any wear and tear on the tracks, and the latter are only used when required. The practical difficulties are, however, considerable. Much extra weight is entailed, and the machine is not usually so good as an armoured car or a tank at either of their special rôles. There is no great difficulty in producing a practical machine of this type for the lighter types of fighting vehicle; it is with the heavier machines that the problem is more difficult. Unfortunately, it is with the latter that it is most needed. The light machines can now travel fast and with little wear and tear on tracks. The "wheel cum track" idea is not, therefore, very promising at present.

All the armoured fighting vehicles have now been described, and the specifications at which we are aiming, or have already reached, have been given, and we can now turn to a consideration of their employment in war. The reasons for disbanding the Armoured Force have already been given in Chapter XIII, and this was followed by a proposal to form armoured brigades instead. Owing to lack of suitable machines in existence, and also to financial stringency, it was decided that no practical trials in this direction would be carried out to start with. Instead, a book was produced in 1929 by the War Office, entitled, " Mechanized and Armoured Formations," which explained the whole policy. The book was popularly called the " Mauve Manual," from the colour of its cover, and it is neither a secret nor confidential document. It is in the nature of a mildly futurist book, and it is probably the first occasion on which a Government Department has been bold enough to issue a book of this nature. As a result, the book has been heavily criticised in some quarters, but also greeted with acclamation in others. Whatever one's own views may be, it is obviously better to have an official policy for the future, even if it is based on untried methods, than to drift with everyone forming his own views. Moreover, the book is in no way dictatorial, and leaves plenty of scope for interpreting the general policy laid down to suit particular occasions as they arise.

It is not proposed to give a résumé of this book in this chapter, but to state briefly the main points and to discuss certain considerations that arise. After describing the vehicles generally, the book considers organisation, one of the main principles being that the units comprising a brigade should be similar in their characteristics, so that they can march and fight together. A Light Armoured Brigade is to consist of two or three light tank battalions with some close-support tanks and an armoured anti-aircraft battery; a regiment of armoured cars being added if the ground and conditions are suitable. A light tank battalion is to have 50 light tanks, so that the brigade may have as many as 150 of these small fighting vehicles.

A medium armoured brigade is to consist of one medium tank battalion, with an establishment of 31 medium tanks, two light tank battalions, some close-support tanks, and an armoured anti-aircraft battery.

Referring to the higher organisation in the army, the book divides the forces into mobile troops and combat troops, and as this division has a very

PRESENT-DAY PROGRESS WITH TANKS. 217

important bearing on the use of armoured fighting vehicles a brief consideration of this point is necessary before passing on to discuss the employment of these armoured brigades.

From the earliest days armies have been divided into mobile troops, who work out ahead, and the slower moving, but harder hitting, combat troops who follow them up. At times the mobile troops have been predominant and the combat troops have been in the nature of camp followers. At other times the mobile troops have fallen largely into disuse; for instance, during the latter days of the Roman Empire the foot soldier was the all-important part of the army, and the mobile troops hardly existed. The pendulum has swung fairly steadily from side to side, but both sides have always existed, and some of the greatest campaigns have been fought when the mobile troops were playing a very important part in the army. In the past these mobile troops have always been light cavalry. This has not, of course, formed the whole work of the cavalry. Heavy cavalry were nearly always used as part of the combat troops; sometimes they had a fair degree of mobility, but it was always much lower than that of the light cavalry who formed the mobile troops. At other times the armour of the heavy cavalry weighed so much that they had less mobility than infantry.

During the last 100 years the work of the light cavalry as the mobile troops of the army has become less important, until it is now practically confined to strategical reconnaissance. They still go out and send in valuable reports on the enemy's movements, but on wide fronts they no longer serve as a really serious threat to his advancing columns. There are many people who think that we are now in a position to resurrect this work of the mobile troops which was of predominant importance in the past by the use of these light armoured brigades.

These brigades can, of course, only operate on ground which is suitable for them; but in most theatres, when the war is one of any magnitude, there is ground over which the enemy must advance which is suitable for their employment. The proposal, therefore, is that the mobile troops shall consist of both cavalry brigades and light armoured brigades, under one commander, the latter being used on the more open ground and the former on ground where the light tank could not operate.

The mobile troops then advance to obtain touch with the enemy, sending armoured cars a long way ahead for this purpose and working in co-operation with the air force. The enemy may be advancing in two or three or more columns, and on his dispositions will depend those of the light armoured brigades and cavalry. As information comes in the Commander of the whole force makes his plans. He may decide to hold off one or more columns while he attacks the remainder, and he will instruct the commander of the mobile troops accordingly. Now cavalry alone, used in the comparatively small numbers which will be available for this work, are not a sufficient threat to the enemy to delay him seriously, but with a light armoured brigade no rôle could be more suitable. The policy of these brigades should be exactly the same as the policy of light cavalry when used for this purpose in the past, namely, to hit weakness and avoid strength. On the march the enemy column is defenceless against an attack by light tanks, which have enough mobility to move round an advanced guard and attack the main body with ease. Hence the enemy will be forced to put out a screen of anti-tank weapons and artillery to protect himself, which will have to take up a position and then leap-frog forward to a second position, the main body moving up by bounds behind them. This work will not only be most exhausting, but exceedingly slow, and the speed of the column may easily be reduced from 15 to 5 miles a day. This power of threatening an advancing column was often referred to by General Sir John Burnett-Stuart, who commanded the 3rd Division, to which the Armoured Force belonged. General Burnett-Stuart used to put it that " An Armoured Force was most formidable when it was at large just below the horizon." The enemy might know that it was there, but he could not tell when an attack might come, or the direction in which it would be delivered. If the enemy took chances and did not use a strong protective screen, the light armoured brigade could advance at high speed, annihilate a portion of the column and clear away before opposition could be organised.

If the enemy did use a strong protective

screen and accepted the fact that he had to move slowly, or took up a defensive position, he should not be attacked by the light brigade; this would be attacking strength, for which it was not equipped, and could not be equipped without losing much mobility. Instead of doing this the light brigade should keep a close watch, and perhaps work round in rear on occasions, cutting communications and effecting demolitions. This would force the enemy to leave detachments to guard important centres on his communications. In this way the enemy column would be greatly retarded and arrive on the battle-field partially exhausted and possibly denuded of important detachments left to guard communications. This would be the rôle of the light armoured brigades, and by this means they might be able to control the enemy movements and enable the commander of the whole force to fight the main battle in a position and under conditions of his own choosing. There is nothing highly imaginary about these proposals, and something of this nature was effected when the Mechanized Force attacked the 3rd Division on Salisbury Plain in 1927, as described in Chapter XIII. It should, however, be particularly noted that for this work a high degree of mobility is required of the vehicles. There is no necessity, either, for any large amount of artillery or for the heavier types of fighting vehicle, because no attack against strong enemy positions is intended.

This action on the part of light armoured brigades would, however, produce counter-action on the part of the enemy, and although, as will be shown later, it is far easier for us to produce armoured forces than for any of our possible enemies, yet they would certainly produce something in the nature of mobile armoured anti-tank weapons. If the enemy went to the expense of constructing them in very large numbers and using them in co-operation with other troops, they would enable the enemy to hold off attacks by light tanks, though his mobility would still be hampered; there would, however, be cases where his defence would depend on a few of these anti-tank weapons, and to attack these the light brigades need close-support guns. They would also need them for defence if attacked by a small number of medium tanks. If attacked by large numbers they would, of course, use their mobility to escape, but it would be difficult for the enemy to know when and where to concentrate his medium tanks to meet these sudden attacks by light tanks. These close-support guns may take the form of a few medium tanks, if they can be made with the necessary mobility, or they may be the close-support tanks which have already been described. In any case it seems reasonably certain that a 3-pdr. gun, mounted on a light and handy track vehicle and fitted with a shield, could be constructed with the necessary mobility; this would advance just behind the light tanks, which would protect them from small-arms fire in rear while it dealt with the anti-tank weapons or medium tanks already referred to. It would, therefore, seem that armoured cars and light tanks, with a few of these close-support guns, and assisted by the air, could resurrect this very important part which was played by the mobile troops in the past.

The administrative side of the problem must not be forgotten. It will be remembered that the Armoured Force on Salisbury Plain presented such a difficult maintenance problem that its mobility was crippled. In this case, however, we have shed all our heavy vehicles which consume such alarming quantities of petrol and oil. The light armoured brigade consists mainly of light tank battalions, and four 30-cwt. lorries carry sufficient petrol and oil to refill one of these battalions after a run of 100 miles. This is not an alarming figure, and on this scale the maintenance problem should be quite feasible.

So far we have only considered the mobile troops and the way in which light armoured brigades can help them, and we have seen that their action may have decisive results on the course of the campaign. We must now consider the action when the combat troops of both sides meet in battle and the way in which the medium armoured brigades can help them. This brigade consists essentially of a medium tank battalion, two light tank battalions to assist the medium tanks, and the close-support tanks for firing high explosive or smoke at anti-tank weapons.

The ground held by the enemy as a main position may be enclosed or open country, or it may contain both types of country. Enclosed country, where there is plenty of cover to conceal anti-tank weapons, is difficult for the advance of medium tanks without heavy artillery support, but is more suitable for an infantry attack. On the other hand, open country, where the concealment of anti-tank weapons is difficult, lends itself to a sweeping attack by a medium armoured brigade. Hence the general proposal is that the latter shall attack the open ground, generally as a surprise from a flank, while the infantry begin to advance against the enemy in the more enclosed ground. An early success by the medium brigade will, of course, greatly assist the infantry, and they may be further assisted by subsequent attacks of the medium brigades further round on the enemy flanks or rear. In this way it is hoped that main battles which took days or weeks to stage in the past may be fought without delay and with decisive results by using the full power of the armour and the mobility of medium brigades.

Unless the enemy has had time to construct wide trenches, the attack by the medium tanks is to be led by the light tanks. They will draw the fire of anti-tank weapons, which are to be at once destroyed by the fire power of the medium and close-support tanks, or, in some cases, screened by smoke from the latter. The light tanks will also scout for the mediums and protect their flanks.

The above gives a very brief and general picture of the employment and attack by medium armoured brigades, and there is no doubt that if attacks of this nature can be carried out successfully they will have an overwhelming effect on the enemy. There are, however, many difficulties to be faced, and they can be painted very forcibly by those who are doubtful about the success of this type of attack in war. They can equally be glossed over by the more extreme tank enthusiasts, and the truth, as usual, probably lies somewhere between the two.

First of all there is the difficulty of the ground. If the ground is all enclosed or mountainous or heavily wooded, the medium brigades cannot be used at all, but it should be remembered that practically all the great and important battles in history have been fought on the plains. Even then, however, the ground may be bumpy and rough, and the medium tanks will bucket badly at speed. Unless the fire from these tanks is accurate they will have no hope against even small numbers of anti-tank weapons, and accurate fire from a rocking platform is difficult. This is largely a matter of training, and mechanical improvements will be introduced to ease the bumping of the tanks; the Tank Corps are improving rapidly in this direction. To what extent this fire will be accurate under the stress of war, when bullets are making a noise like sledge hammers on the outside of the tanks, and splash and dust obscure the vision, is difficult to say; nor can one judge to what extent the tank commanders will be able to control the fire from the guns and machine-guns in this tumult in the forefront of the battle, but these, again, will be greatly assisted by careful peace time training.

Then there is the difficulty of seeing the target

and spotting the anti-tank weapons. It is wrong to judge these matters by war time experience, because we have made great strides since then, but one can still apply the war conditions to the new tanks. Certainly during the war the very great difficulty of spotting anti-tank weapons from tanks was most marked, and there were a great many cases of tanks being knocked out without any of the crew knowing where the firing had come from. It can be done fairly well, of course, under peace conditions, but here again the excitement in the forefront of the battle makes it all much more difficult in war. The trouble with " splash " entering the tank, which was explained in Chapter IV, made observation difficult during the war. Much progress is being made in eliminating splash entirely in modern tanks. When this is achieved it will greatly assist observation and the spotting of anti-tank weapons. There will, therefore, be improvement in this direction, as well as in the development of accurate fire, but the difficulty of subduing concealed anti-tank weapons before they have themselves knocked out the tanks should not be minimised or forgotten.

Then there is the question of the provision of covering fire from machine-guns and artillery. Surprise or semi-independent attacks delivered by medium armoured brigades from a flank are very difficult to support by covering fire. They will, of course, gain by the speed and surprise of the attack, but they will also definitely lose by the lack of strong covering fire. Medium tanks carry the means of providing their own close-support fire, to some extent, anl it is on this and on the fire of the close-support tanks that they will mainly have to depend.

Finally, we come to a difficulty over the question of rallying, and here again General Burnett-Stuart used to put the point very clearly when discussing the tactics of the Armoured Force on Salisbury Plain. When tanks are attacking with infantry they can rally on or behind the captured position, because the infantry are advancing and mopping up and will protect the tanks. But medium brigades attacking independently of infantry cannot possibly rally on the ground over which they have assaulted; if they do so they will be shot at by guns which they have passed by or by guns which the enemy have rushed up, and they may have very heavy casualties. In this case, therefore, medium brigades must either pass right through and rally in concealment or safety beyond, or they must return after their assault to the safety of our own lines. In very open country this is not of much consequence, because the assault will have destroyed all enemy resistance; but there is plenty of closer country where considerable numbers of infantry and guns will lie concealed and will be in no way damaged, either morally or physically, by the charge of a limited number of tanks over that area. This point was well illustrated by our medium tanks when they were endeavouring to co-operate with cavalry in the semi-mobile warfare towards the end of the war. The cavalry would be held up by machine-gun fire coming from a certain area; the medium tanks would therefore sweep through that area; they would kill a few men and the machine-guns would be silenced. They could not, however, remain in the area, or enemy field guns would range on to them, and they had to continue the sweep round back to our lines; but as soon as they did this the machine-guns came to life again and repelled the advancing cavalry. The solution in this case would have been a few dismounted men working forward with the tanks to mop up.

Many difficulties have been referred to in the above remarks, but they must not be taken as unsurmountable. Improved tanks will help accuracy of fire and observation, and make strong artillery support less necessary; increased numbers of light tanks will assist in searching the ground and make the assault more effective in subduing the enemy. In these, and many other ways, the medium armoured brigades can be made more effective in the future. The question, however, of any extensive tactical trials on the ground has been rendered impossible by the financial situation, and there is no prospect at present of obtaining these larger armoured formations for trial. Instead, the tank battalions at home are being equipped for trials with some medium and some light tanks, and thereby formed into miniature medium armoured brigades.

In schemes and trials these units are generally being used in a less ambitious manner than the semi-independent attack of the larger and more powerful medium brigades. They are normally used to overwhelm the enemy resistance on a portion of the main position, with the infantry advancing at the earliest possible moment to mop it up. These tactics have war experience behind them in principle; they are simple and very clearly explained in the Tank and Armoured Car Training Manual, and are clearly understood by everyone; also, they eliminate most of the difficulties which accompany the more independent use of the medium armoured brigades. Until such time as we have progressed further and been able to try out this more independent rôle, it is by the co-operation of these mixed tank battalions and infantry that we are the most likely to achieve rapid success when attacking main positions.

It must not be thought that the light armoured brigades will take no part in this main battle. As the main bodies close on each other the light brigades and the cavalry will withdraw in rear or to a flank. Then, as the infantry advance and the medium tanks attack with them or from a flank, the light brigades will be moving still further round on the flanks. They will still follow the policy of hitting the weak and avoiding the strength. If the enemy throws back a flank with anti-tank defence to keep them off, they must move further round still. The enemy will be threatened with an encircling movement by the light brigades, and he may seriously weaken his defences in endeavouring to prolong his flank. If he does this it will greatly assist our main attack. If he does not do this there is every chance of light brigades working round, disorganising his rear areas and communications and spreading despondency in his army. Harassing the enemy during his advance and working round his flank in the main battle were the two well-established duties of the light cavalry in the past; if this work has been less prominent in late years, due to the fact that cavalry have less striking power, these seems no reason why it should not be resurrected with redoubled force by the use of light armoured brigades on the good ground, assisted by cavalry brigades on the difficult ground.

CHAPTER XVII.

ARMOURED CARRIERS AND THE USE OF UNARMOURED VEHICLES.

IN the last chapter only one way of assisting the combat troops was considered, namely, by the use of medium tanks or medium armoured brigades. It will be remembered that the second group of mechanical vehicles referred to at the beginning of the last chapter contains the armoured carriers, and these can render very great assistance to the infantry battalions in many ways.

We will start with the armoured machine-gun carrier, because this is by far the most important. This machine consists of a light, low and inconspicuous vehicle on tracks. The engine and transmission are commercial motor components, so that these machines could be made rapidly and in large numbers in war, and their price is cheap, in peace being about £450 for one machine. The armour is proof against armour-piercing bullets in front, and gives a fair degree of protection on the flanks. The machine carries two men (including the driver) and one machine-gun and 3,000 rounds of ammunition; it can travel at 15 miles an hour on the level, and has a fairly good cross-country performance, being able to climb steep slopes and work its way in and out or over most natural obstacles. It is, however, very bumpy when travelling over rough ground, owing to its very short length, and although the gun is so mounted that it can fire on the move, it cannot fire accurately and can only sprinkle an area unless passing slowly over a smooth piece of ground. Two men, are, of course, quite inadequate for maintaining a machine-gun in action for a long period; for instance, when the machine-gun is being used in defence the complete detachment is essential. To carry the additional personnel and some extra ammunuition an unarmoured trailer has been added which is towed behind the machine. This reduces very considerably both the speed and the cross-country performance of the vehicle, though the men in the trailer can jump off and assist over bad places.

These machines were issued for trial in 1929, and the instructions were that they merely replaced the horse-drawn limbers by a more efficient means of transport, and that the machine-guns were normally to be fired from the ground. The idea was that as the vehicle had some armour protection it could approach closer to the front, and if necessary, the additional men in the unarmoured trailer could drop off and creep up and join the gun a little later.

In Chapter XI it was explained that the original idea suggested by the inventors of these small machines was that large numbers should be available, and that they should practically become mechanical infantry. This, of course, was a proposal for the eventual future, but the immediate proposal made by the Army swung in the other direction.

No one will deny the general value of covering machine-gun fire, but it does not begin to solve the problem which is the main source of all the infantryman's trouble in the attack. This, of course, is the concealed enemy machine-gun, and unless some men can advance behind armour protection for the last few hundred yards to locate and knock out these concealed enemy machine-guns, no further advance will be made, in many cases, in spite of all the machine-gun covering fire in the world. There was, therefore, a general demand in the army that the policy should swing back towards the original idea, and that the machines should be so designed that, at any rate, some of them could definitely advance close up against the enemy and spot enemy machine-guns and subdue them by their fire from very close range. It was therefore decided that a number of these machines in some battalions should be used and tried out in this way, and they were called " infighters." They need rather higher armour in front for this work, but are generally the same as the machine already described. The trailer, of course, is not used for this work, and the crew is limited to two men.

The general idea is that these infighters shall work up in front in close co-operation with, or under the orders of the Commanders of the rifle companies. When a Rifle Company is held up, the commander of (we will say) a platoon of four of these infighters makes a plan with the company commander. He decides, perhaps, to rush forward 50 yards to a bank which will give him some cover, and over which he can fire with his machine-guns. While he is doing this, or as a result of this action, the infantry advance again. This process is continued, the infighters sneaking forward, avoiding bad obstacles but making full use of all available cover from the ground; this will save the machines from the fire of anti-tank weapons and the personnel from possible casualties from small-arm fire due to splash through loopholes. Finally, the centres of enemy resistance are accurately located and his machine-guns brought under heavy fire from the infighters at close range, which either subdues them or enables the rifle company to do so.

When the position has been captured and it is desired to hold it defensively for a time, the machine-guns require the remainder of the detachment. These can either walk up, carrying the ammunition, or they can be provided with a second machine in which to come up when required. In any case the gun can be dismounted from the infighter and used defensively on the ground, freeing the machine to fetch up more ammunition; or if suitable cover is available the gun can remain mounted on the machine and fire over a mound or bank; this latter case would probably be exceptional unless the position was only to be held for a short time.

How many of these infighters we shall find necessary for this work is difficult to say, and practical trials will have to guide us. This work may lead us to having some infighters as part of every rifle company, replacing the light automatics, and only a smaller number of machine-guns being used in the machine-gun company for the longer range covering fire. In the attack the long range covering fire is only there to help in putting the rifle companies on to the objective, and has never been outstandingly successful; if we can put the companies in more effectively by using the machine-guns as infighters the longer range covering fire is less necessary, and has in any case always been done far more effectively by artillery.

These, of course, are only possible suggestions for the future. Looking still further ahead, it does not seem so very impossible that the original proposals may eventually come true. Why should not each pair of fighting men have a small infighter machine, leaving the administrative personnel of the battalion to follow on in six-wheel lorries? One of the finest armies that the world has ever known was commanded by Genghiz Khan, and with it he conquered the whole of Asia and the Middle East. The whole army was mounted, each man having three horses; when it came to Mountain Warfare or a siege, the necessary number of men dismounted and fought on foot. Why should we not have a highly mobile army of this nature and fight on foot, when necessary? When the ground is suitable, what sort of defence is going to stop large numbers of infighters advancing at, say, 10 miles an hour? These speculations, however, are only intended to stimulate ideas for the future. We are progressing very fast, and every month some improvements are made to these mechanical vehicles, and we will gradually build up our future policy on sound foundations.

This work in connection with Armoured Machine-gun Carriers is possibly the most important of all the work on which we are engaged. So long as the machines are left at the present reasonable figure of cost, it enables us to equip all battalions without finding the money by cutting down something else, because they replace existing horse-drawn equipment. In war the battalions will have some means of assistance against the concealed machine-guns, in all circumstances. When they are on advanced guard there will be many cases where tanks will not be available to help them, but they will still have their infighters to assist them. Then, again, when attacking a main position there may be many battalions attacking against an enclosed portion of the front, and all the tanks may be employed to assist the advance on more suitable tank country. Here again these armoured carriers and infighters may save the battalions very great casualties and enable them to advance in a way which they could never hope to do without them.

A further use for armoured carriers lies in the employment of a small tractor which is practically the same as the Armoured Machine-gun Carrier, and is being tried for towing the 3.7-inch Howitzer as a close-support weapon. In this way it replaces many mules which are normally used for this work. When this weapon is carried as pack loads on the mules it can of course, traverse ground and narrow tracks on which no vehicle could move, but on average ground the small tractor has proved very suitable. It enables the gun to be taken up to places which would be far too exposed to enemy fire for mules, and often enables the gunners to carry out their work in very close support to the leading infantry. The Howitzer is carried on a small tracked trailer.

Another way in which armoured carriers can assist the army is in their use as vehicles for smoke producing devices. Smoke has been used from the earliest days to assist miilitary operations, and it was revived early in the war, as a smoke rifle grenade, to give the infantryman some means of masking and then attacking machine-guns. With the introduction of tanks smoke became of great importance, and it has had considerable use ever since. At present we are trying small armoured carriers carrying light mortars for throwing smoke and high explosive bombs. These vehicles are similar to the armoured machine-gun carriers, and can creep up close behind the infantry, due to their armour protection, and they can, therefore, work in very close co-operation with the leading troops.

Another armoured carrier that is being tried is a similar type of vehicle which is intended for producing a long bank of smoke to screen a flank or conceal a movement of troops rather than to mask a particular weapon or a nest of machine-guns. The vehicle carries no mortar, but produces the smoke in one of two ways. In one type Sulphonic Acid is dripped into the exhaust, causing a dense bank of smoke to be emitted therefrom; this method was used by the Navy during the war. An excellent smoke screen is produced, but the vehicle itself may often be a conspicuous and easy target for the enemy while making the screen. The other type is fitted with a tube, and smoke candles are dropped through this tube on to the ground. As they drop a delay action fuse is actuated and the candle ignites later. The screen produced is not so good as that made by the sulphonic acid, but as the smoke does not appear till later, the machine does not draw so much attention to itself in action.

Armoured carriers are also being tried as a means of enabling anti-aircraft guns and machine-guns to advance and come into action against low-flying aeroplanes in places where they might come under enemy fire from the ground, and also to give them some protection from the fire of the aeroplanes. Many other uses can, of course, be suggested for armoured carriers, and this group of vehicles is one which may increase considerably in general use in the future.

The remaining group contains the unarmoured mechanical vehicles. Most of the work of this group is administrative, such as bringing up shells and rations, and the vehicles used for such purposes have all been described in Chapter X. There are, however, some definite tactical uses in the employment of some of these unarmoured vehicles. The most important use lies in the mechanization of the first-line transport of fighting units. It is often necessary to move units, such as infantry battalions, as rapidly as possible, and lorries or buses are an obvious means of doing so. It will be remembered that General Gallieni moved large numbers of troops in Paris taxi-cabs in 1914, when he initiated the attack on the German right flank which led to the battle of the Marne. Such moves are, however, much handicapped by the fact that the horse-drawn transport which carries the ammunition and food, etc., of these units cannot accompany the lorries or buses. Thus, although the units arrive early on the battle-field, they are deprived of certain essential first-line transport.

With a view to overcoming this difficulty we have carried out a good deal of experimental work in mechanizing this transport and trying it out. The vehicles must have a good cross-country capacity, and be capable of traversing any ground over which horse-drawn transport can operate. So far most of our trials have been carried out with 30-cwt. six-wheel lorries. They have been very successful on the whole, but it is not yet certain that their cross-country capacity is sufficiently high. If it is not considered high enough, other methods will be tried, and it is certain that mechanical transport can be devised that will travel anywhere that a limbered wagon or A.T. Cart can move.

In the design of these vehicles it will be essential to use commercial components for the engine, transmission, etc., and very desirable to use a commercial chassis complete; but there is no reason why a special body to suit service requirements should not be used. The normal lorry body of the commercial vehicle is high and conspicuous, and more suitable bodies can easily be devised and used for this first line of transport.

If a commander has mechanized first-line transport for even a portion of his combat troops it gives him very great advantages. The difficulty of moving troops by lorry, which was referred to above, disappears at once when we have this mechanical transport. There is seldom any great difficulty in collecting the necessary lorries or buses to move the men, and the first-line mechanical transport can then accompany them. If four-wheel lorries or buses are used the troops will be tied to the roads, but if six-wheel lorries can be obtained, then a certain degree of cross-country movement becomes possible. With three-ton six-wheel lorries, 35 vehicles are required to move the personnel of an infantry battalion which has mechanized first-line transport.

The possession of troops with mechanized first-line transport leads to a temptation to send them ahead to meet the enemy; it should, however, be remembered that even if a commander has a force in which half the combat troops possess this extra mobility, it is of little value to send them ahead and give the enemy a hard but indecisive blow if the remainder of the combat troops are too far away to profit by the result and complete the victory. At times there are strong advantages in sending a portion of these more mobile combat troops ahead to secure some important tactical feature, such as a river crossing, but their work should not be confused with that of the mobile troops. The normal employment should be to keep these mobile portions of the combat troops to a flank, or in the rear, and to use their mobility to bring them round on the enemy flank, as a surprise, at the same time that the enemy is being pinned to the ground or attacked by the remainder of the combat troops.

It should, of course, be remembered that the lorries employed for this work are very vulnerable and a very easy target for any machine-guns which the enemy can rush up and conceal in ambush. The movement must, therefore, usually be covered by cavalry or light tanks. It is also usually necessary for the men to dismount from the lorries well in rear and approach on foot, because the lorries are conspicuous targets, but even then an outflanking movement can often be carried out far more quickly in this way than by men marching on foot.

There is one other direction in which unarmoured mechanical vehicles have rendered assistance tactically, and that is in connection with the use of small light unarmoured vehicles for scouting. The origin of the work was as follows:—Brigadier R. J. Collins was often discussing the necessity for a small vehicle to replace the horse when talking about reconnaissance work for the Armoured Force, and Major-General H. H. S. Knox also referred to the fact that for scouting work it might be not only possible, but advantageous, to use unarmoured vehicles. It then occurred to me that a very light car, like the Austin Seven, with suitable reinforcing and a special body, might be just what we required. This was in July, 1928, and in

The Austin Scout for Cavalry Work.

order to save the unavoidable delays of official action I wrote at once to the Austin firm, and they kindly offered to lend me a chassis for trials. It arrived in a few days and we fitted it up in the 17th Field Company Workshops. A piece of ash about three inches square was fixed just under the carden shaft to save it from damage when passing over mounds or ditches; handles were fixed in various places, and all unnecessary weight removed. There was no windscreen, of course, and special seats were provided. The driver had a normal bucket seat, but the gunner on his left had a seat with a small platform behind it. Thus the gunner could either sit low down and be as inconspicuous as the driver, or he could sit on the platform at the back of his seat, in which case he could see over low hedges. He could also stand on this platform, in which case he steadied himself by a thin steel pole which fitted into sockets for the purpose, and in this position he was rather higher than a man on a horse and had a good view for scouting over hedges or bushes. The sides of the car were quite open, so that both men could slip out and throw themselves on the ground, if necessary.

Being extremely light, the machine had a surprisingly good cross-country performance, and after a little training the two men could " heave " it over quite difficult obstacles. When working in pairs the four men could carry one vehicle at a time over almost any obstacle. The great advantage of this machine was, of course, the high speed over roads or tracks for long distances.

Medium or long-distance reconnaissances could be carried out in incredibly short times. The speed, however, fell off very rapidly cross-country, especially when it had to pick its way. Generally speaking, it was a most useful adjunct to cavalry, especially in saving horseflesh for medium distance reconnaissance. It could do some scouting, but for short distance work and for scouting, especially on rough ground, the horse had, of course, every advantage over the machine.

This vehicle became known as the Austin scout, and it has sometimes been stated that this was a misnomer, and that it was really only capable of bringing back news rapidly. The capabilities of a machine of this nature depend, of course, entirely on the ground, but on suitable ground there is nothing to prevent it from scouting, though this is not its main rôle. The idea was that the gunner would have a rifle, or possibly a light automatic. He would thus be better armed than cavalry if an enemy cavalry patrol was suddenly encountered. Then, if the car came under fire and was unable to escape to cover, the men would tumble out on to the ground. If it was destroyed the loss would be no greater than that of two horses, and the vulnerable parts present a far smaller target than even one horse. There is, therefore, no reason why a machine of this nature should not be used for scouting on suitable ground, when necessary.

CHAPTER XVIII.

CONCLUSION.

A PERFECTLY fair criticism which may have occurred to the reader at this stage is that many of the discussions in the book have been argued as though we were well supplied with armoured fighting vehicles and could count on fighting an enemy who possessed none or only a few. For instance, in Chapter XVI it was suggested that the enemy would have to use a screen of anti-tank weapons and guns to provide protection for his combat troops against our light armoured brigades, whereas it might be argued that the right course for the enemy would be to equip himself also with light brigades to hunt ours and chase them away. That any enemy whom we may fight is likely to have some armoured fighting vehicles is obvious, but it is not at all likely, at present, that he will have armoured formations and fighting vehicles on the scale which has been discussed in this book.

Our most likely wars at present are against semi-civilised people for the protection of our foreign possessions and such enemies are not in the least likely to possess anything serious in this way. If we turn to consider possible commitments in a European war due to the Locarno Pact, we find that our opponents would be faced with very real difficulties compared to ourselves in producing an army well equipped with armoured formations and fighting vehicles. All European countries have long land frontiers, and it is the defence of these frontiers that is their main concern. It is quite easy to turn round and explain that a small army well equipped with fighting vehicles will be far more efficient for attacking and eventually destroying the invader's main columns, but this is at present quite unproved, and while the small mechanized army was thus engaged, some of these enemy columns would be invading the land, destroying property and obtaining a hold on the country. Even if the soldiers were agreed, it is possible that the civilians who pay for the army in peace time would demand a large man-power army for protective duties under these conditions.

If it were possible for a large continental army to change into a smaller but still fairly large mechanized army, the change would have obvious advantages; but this is not possible without a very great increase in financial expenditure, which no country is at present likely to face. In Chapter XI we saw how our own Regular Army could change to a mechanized army without being greatly diminished in size, and certainly possessing far more fighting value in a great war. This could be achieved because our men are highly paid and by reducing the numbers a great saving could be effected to offset the outlay on mechanical machines and their maintenance. With a Foreign Army only small savings are effected by reducing the number of conscript soldiers, and consequently a very big reduction in the size of the army would be needed if it was to be equipped on a modern scale with armoured formations and fighting vehicles. It is this reduction that continental armies show no sign at present of favouring or accepting.

We are, therefore, in a unique position, and that is why we are forging ahead with ideas and experiments in mechanization. Just imagine what would have happened in 1914 if we had possessed light armoured brigades to harass and delay two or three of the enemy main columns, and backed up by combat troops consisting of mechanized or armoured formations or bodies consisting largely of small tanks, as suggested in Chapter XI, and all at a cost which did not exceed that of our present small expeditionary force. The whole strategical situation would have changed, and there is no doubt that the possession of such a force would give us the balance of power in any continental conflict.

It may be asked why we do not proceed at once and carry this out, and the answer is that our most likely wars are, as we have already suggested, in hot countries for the protection of our foreign possessions. Owing to the ground that is likely to be met under these conditions, and the probable temperatures, we are not sure at present whether we shall be able to obtain equal value from these machines. We are, therefore, quite rightly and wisely moving slowly, even though it is faster than any other nation. We do not want to have two armies, one for a possible but remote continental war and the other for the everyday needs on foreign service. All machines have, therefore, to be tested and tried out for both purposes. That we shall succeed, to a large extent, is certain, but it will take time.

In this connection, India is often referred to as the stumbling block which is holding us back in all progress. This may, or may not, have been true in the past, but it is certainly not true to-day. India is forging ahead with the use of six-wheel lorries, both for administrative purposes and for artillery traction, and is only awaiting the development of suitable machines to try out small tanks and armoured carriers. It is no fault of India that the designers at home ignored her special needs in mobility and temperature restrictions for many years; but all this work is now in hand, and there is no doubt that India will progress fast in the near future.

Although a general outline has been given in this book showing some of the ways in which we are aiming at building up our existing arms into a mechanized army, and suggesting the types of machine that are needed, it should remain quite clear that we are still in the very early days of mechanization. We are at present groping in the dark, and new types of machine are constantly appearing with capabilities which were previously thought to be unobtainable. Many statements have been made in this book as regards the general capabilities of machines; for instance, it has been stated that the machines used for the more highly mobile troops must be comparatively short and light, and that the heavier tanks need a great deal of maintenance work if used for long and fairly continuous running. That the heavier tanks will use a great deal of petrol and oil is probably inevitable, and this is bound to limit their use for very long-range work, owing to the difficulty of supplying these necessities, but the other views expressed as regards the size and capabilities of machines may quite well need radical alterations as development proceeds. The general picture that has been given about the various types and sizes of machines and their cost and performance has been based on the present-day knowledge of what we know can be made and produced; no attempt has, however, been made to look a long way ahead mechanically and envisage machines which can put up a performance far beyond anything which we know about at present, and there would probably be very little value in doing so.

In the work of development new suggestions are constantly being tried. For instance, there is now a civilian invention for a new type of track. Instead of joining the track plates together with a pin joint, which invariably leads to rapid wear and tear, the plates are joined by a connecting piece, with the ends embedded in rubber in each track plate. Thus the tension between the track plates is transmitted by this connecting piece to compression on the rubber. As the track passes round the sprocket or idler wheel in front, the rubber distorts; there is, therefore, no friction, and pins which wear out and cause trouble are eliminated. The life of these tracks has been proved to be very high, and far ahead of anything which we have at present. This type of track has been placed on the market by Roadless Traction, Ltd., for use with Ford and other commercial tractors, and it may mark a great advance in tracks for tanks.

In this and many other ways the tanks will gradually develop and alter their form. Whether the fighting vehicles of the future combat troops will take the form of fairly large tanks or larger numbers of small tanks, is hard to say. It is easy to argue on both sides. Perhaps, on the whole, the arguments in favour of smaller and more numerous tanks outweigh the arguments for the larger machines. In our wars with nature to establish civilisation, we have never had any difficulty in dealing with large animals, however fierce they might be; the mammoths were eliminated quite easily, but the locusts have defied our most scientific attempts to destroy them.

It can also be argued that we are overdoing the use of armour, and that lighter, cheaper and more mobile machines, using nothing but a shield, would be far better value. Armour of some kind has always been used in war; the Roman soldier had his shield as armour, but he kept it to a reasonable size and weight, and warded off enemy blows from the direction in which they were coming. He did not consider it necessary to have an all-round shield to ward off surprise blows coming from any direction. In the same way, we might equip our fighting vehicles with a shield which they would use to swing round to the required direction and ward off the enemy fire; this would enable us to have larger numbers of lighter and handier fighting vehicles, compared to the number and type available if we insist on all-round protection. Moreover, a shield might be made of heavier armour plate than we could afford to use for covering the whole of a vehicle, and thus provide protection against the lighter types of anti-tank weapons.

It is often suggested that a modern army which makes full use of fighting vehicles should be modelled on the Navy. There are, of course, points of similarity between a navy and a mechanized army, but the parallel does not go very far. On the sea a more powerful ship can sink an inferior vessel in a few minutes without any doubt as to the issue, provided the two are more or less equally efficiently equipped and manned. On land there is no such parallel. The earth is not a flat plain like the sea, and concealment is generally possible; the result is that the most powerful tank ever built may easily be knocked out if fired at from close range by a comparatively small but concealed anti-tank gun. It is true that smoke screens and darkness and the use of torpedoes and mines may enable the smaller vessels to hold their own for a time, but in the end the capital ship wins on the sea. On land a certain degree of supremacy could be obtained by using more powerfully armoured tanks as a surprise, as suggested in Chapter IX, but the gun will easily defeat the armour in the end, when the latter has to be transported cross-country by mechanical means. Owing to the very different conditions on the sea compared with the land, the general policy has been to pit armour against guns, but such a policy would be fatal in the army. It is by the use of speed and mobility and a reasonable use of armour that we shall succeed on the land, and our work of development is not very greatly assisted by a comparison with the Navy in this direction.

In connection with this work of development, there is one very important point which is apt to be overlooked. Everyone in charge of experimental work is seeking after the ideal; this is as it should be, but it may lead to a state where there is no finality, and no stage where the troops are equipped with the good, even if it is not the best. In the past there were definite limitations. For instance, it was quite reasonable to lay down that the Field Gun was to be the best weapon that could be drawn by a six-horse team. There was no way of increasing the power of the horses, and this gave one a definite limitation. The result was that a degree of finality was soon reached, and the troops equipped with an excellent weapon, even though experimental work continued. With mechanization it is very difficult to lay down any limitation of this nature. Hence everyone asks for better and more expensive machines, and no degree of finality is reached. What is required is that experimental work shall continue till something that is "good" is produced. Then the troops can be

CONCLUSION. 251

equipped and minor improvements continue every year. At the same time the experimental work continues, and when a definite stage of a much improved weapon is reached the equipment is changed, if finance will permit. If not, then the new design is completed to the last detail, and in the event of war munition factories can make the improved design at once without any delay. Unless the work goes forward in definite stages in this way, there is every danger that when war occurs the munition factories may have to start by manufacturing the existing patterns, because, although the experimental work is much ahead of this, there is no type that has been thoroughly tested out and with which it is safe to go into production.

It is, of course, very difficult to suggest any limitations to which we can work. Possibly financial cost is the best; many people object to considering the cost as a vital part of the specification of a weapon, but finance represents labour and material, and is the easiest figure to use. After all, the type and number of vehicles and weapons with which we go to war are exactly what we can afford to buy in peace. We do not know enough of the mechanical possibilities of tanks to say so yet, but we might reach a stage when we can say that the light tank is to be the best tank that can be produced for " X " pounds. This would give one a definite limitation, like the six-horse team for the field gun, and enable us to concentrate on that type of tank and produce a really good article which was as near as possible to the requirements in the

General Staff specification. Without some limitation of this nature, everyone naturally wants more power, more speed, a steadier platform, etc., etc., and there is no finality by stages.

To choose the right moment to go into production and equip the troops needs great experience and a wide mechanical engineering knowledge. This will come with our improved mechanical engineering organisation referred to in Chapter XV. Without a highly efficient technical staff of this nature, this and many other equally important points will be muddled, and we shall never get the small and efficient regular army, making full use of mechanical assistance, which is our aim.

Again, there are writers who consider that the whole movement in this direction is a temporary phase, and that anti-tank weapons will be developed which will set us back where we were. It is agreed that anti-tank weapons are at present very undeveloped, and that they will always be a constant threat to tanks; for that matter, anti-tank mines are an equally serious threat; but most of the arguments pointing out that armoured fighting vehicles will be eliminated by these means are based on the use of highly developed anti-tank methods against the existing types and numbers of fighting vehicles, and against their present method of employment. How do the anti-tank enthusiasts propose to protect a Division on the march which is attacked by large numbers of fast tanks? The answer to the whole problem is that an army must have both tanks and anti-tank weapons. There are some

CONCLUSION. 253

conditions under which a portion of the army can expect to be able to resist all tank attacks by the use of anti-tank weapons, and there are others under which it will be very vulnerable to tank attacks, in spite of its anti-tank weapons. The successful commanders will be those who effectively combine the defensive use of anti-tank weapons with the offensive use of tanks under suitable conditions, and who are lucky enough to have enough tanks to be able to bring this about.

Whether we like it or not, we must progress in this way. It is forced on us, for one thing, by the progress made among some of our wilder neighbours who live on the borders of our foreign possessions. Twenty years ago they had few rifles and were mainly armed with hand weapons; to-day they have plenty of rifles and ammunition, in many instances, so that whereas we had the necessary ascendency over them in the past by the mere possession of rifles, we can now only obtain this ascendency by the use of all modern weapons and the assistance of the Air Force. These modern weapons need roads and communications for keeping them supplied, etc., and hence it is often stated that war in this modern form is much slower than before, because the roads have often to be constructed as we advance, and this is slow work. The statement, however, is very misleading. If it means that Lord Roberts could advance much more rapidly against the unarmed Afghans with an army that practically only needed rifles and a very limited amount of ammunition, the statement is true, but that type of lightly equipped army could make no headway against the armed tribes of to-day. The irregular force living in its own country and scattering in front of opposition is a very difficult enemy to defeat, and regular troops who are only equally well armed have a very up-hill task against them. The advance of a modern army against them is admittedly slow, but it is quicker than any attempt to meet such a foe without the necessary ascendency over him in equipment. In the past we pitted the rifle against the spear; we must now endeavour to pit armoured vehicles against the rifle, and aim at using cross-country vehicles for supply purposes without being too tied to roads.

In all this work we shall progress most rapidly by building up on our present army. There are those who would wish to see a small separate army installed, using nothing but modern machines and methods, and that as this army developed and grew the old army would gradually die. Granted that it is difficult to re-mould an existing army, with all its vested interests, and that it is easier in some ways to start afresh, yet it is natural that the latter method would be bitterly opposed by the old army. The feeling that one is drifting out of date is most demoralising, and there is no doubt that the right method is to modernise existing arms rather than to form new ones. The army is at present quite ready to accept change and progress, more so probably than at any previous stage in history.

These views are in no way intended as a criticism of the formation and existence of the Royal Tank

Corps. This new Corps was necessary, both during the war and afterwards, to further a new weapon and develop the use of tanks. Starting with no traditions earlier than the war, the Royal Tank Corps has raised units which are now second to none in the army in their soldierly qualities, games, education and general efficiency. They have shown us that men can become greasy and grubby in tanks and still produce the finest soldiers in peace and war. Let the older Corps and Regiments copy them and keep up this standard which the Tank Corps has set when some of them in turn have to become greasy and grubby in fighting vehicles.

It is curious to notice how often we need to look back in considering points that arise to-day in connection with the progress that we are making with mechanization. For instance, it was a great assistance when considering the very vital engineer and repair organisation to look back and see " how we did it in the War." Then again, with new developments it is often possible to find some experience which can be obtained at no cost from the past. If the anti-tank mines become a serious threat to tanks, and we are considering methods of overcoming them, it is useful to know what we thought about it and tried in this direction during or just after the war. Even the minor devices, such as sledges, for bringing up supplies to the rallying points, and grapnels for removing barbed wire, might quite well be needed again in a future war. It is, perhaps, inevitable but unfortunate that there is no record to-day of most of this type of work which was carried out during the war and immediately afterwards. A brief survey of this work of development has been given in this book as the history of the fighting vehicles was traced, and for this, if for no other reason, there may be some value in this book as a record.

There are many other examples which could be given of ways in which we experimented during or just after the war, such as with petrol-electric transmission and with swimming tanks, and it is sometimes thought that we are not now carrying out sufficient experimental work in these and other directions. Such is far from being the case. The Mechanical Warfare Board at the War Office has a stupendous programme of work in hand. Only the more urgent work can be carried out at present, though every suggestion is considered and all these important points kept in mind. Much progress is being made in many directions which is the envy of many other nations.

In what direction the general policy of mechanization will be led in the eventual future is as unknown as it is interesting to discuss. There is however, a policy which has governed the use of armies from the earliest days, and which can be applied equally to armies which use armoured fighting vehicles. This has already been described in Chapter XVI, and consists of dividing the army into mobile and combat troops, using the former to push ahead for reconnaissance and to control the enemy movements, and the latter to hit him when he has been manœuvred into the right position, while the mobile troops attack the flanks and then pursue. With our knowledge as it stands at present, it is the light tanks that will be of such great assistance to the mobile troops in this rôle, while the medium tanks, assisted by light tanks for scouting, must be ready, as a more mobile portion of the combat troops, to deal a heavy blow at the enemy main body and pave the way for the infantry assault. The latter, if assisted by sufficient small and inconspicuous fighting machines or armoured carriers, which can take part in the dog fight, may themselves achieve greater mobility than the infantry of the past, and far greater power in the attack. This is an old, simple and well-tried policy, and it is difficult at present to see any necessity to depart from it in the future.

Our general progress in this direction is ahead of that of all other armies, and practically the whole army is not only ready, but eager, to change and progress still faster, if it were possible. This spirit of progress in the army appears to be a new feature, born as a result of the war; long may it remain.

In this book an endeavour has been made to describe the progress we have made in the first 15 years of mechanization. One wonders what progress will be made in the next 15 years.

APPENDIX GIVING PARTICULARS AND (

WAR

	Number of Machines produced up to 31st December, 1918.	Thickness of Armour Plate in m.m. over vital parts.	Total weight in tons. Fighting Trim.	Overall length in Feet.	Engine.	Petrol consumption. miles per gallon.	Circuit of action in miles on one fill.
Mark I Tank.	Male 75 Female 75	8	26	26	6 Cyl. Daimler 105 H.P. at 1,000 Revs.	½	23
Mark IV Tank.	Male 420 Female 595	12	28	26	ditto	½	35
Mark V. Tank.	Male 200 Female 200	12 14 in places	29	26	6 Cyl. Ricardo 150 H.P. at 1,200 Revs.	½	45
Mark V** Tank.	Male 1 Female 0	12	35	32	6 Cyl. Ricardo 225 H.P. at 1,200 revs.	⅓	67
Mark VIII Tank.	7	12 16 in places	37	34	12 Cyl. Ricardo or Liberty 300 H.P.	¼	55
Medium A Tank.	200	12 14 in places	14	20	Two 45 H.P. Tylor at 1,000 Revs.	1	80
Medium B Tank.	45	ditto	18	23	4 Cyl. Ricardo 100 H.P. at 1,200 Revs.	¾	65
Medium C Tank.	0	ditto	20	26	6 Cyl. Ricardo 150 H.P. at 1,200 Revs.	⅞	120

MODERN E(

Vickers Medium Tank Mk. II.		12	17½	90 H.P. 8 Cyl. Armstrong Siddeley	1½	130
Lanchester 6-Wheel Armoured Car		6	17	45 H.P.	6½	200
30-Cwt. 6-Wheel Lorry		3½	16	About 16 H.P.	10	120
3-Ton 6-Wheel Lorry		7	20	About 27 H.P.	5	80

NOTES. (1) The Obstacle-crossing capacity cannot be expressed in a table gear ratio in the above machines will enable them to climb a this, and about 30 degrees is usually the limit.
(2) Circuit of action means the total distance that the machine
(3) Modern Fighting Vehicles are proof against armour piercing
(4) Light Tanks, Armoured Carriers and Support Tanks are de present for any figures to be given in this table.

CAPABILITIES OF VARIOUS MACHINES.

TANKS.

Armament		Ammunition		Maximum speed on level. Miles per hour.	Clear Gap in ft. which can be crossed.	Height of obstacle in ft. which can be surmounted	Number in Crew.	Depth of water in feet fordable.
Gun.	Machine Guns.	Gun Rds.	S.A.A.					
Male 2 6-pdr.	3	Male 324	6,000	4	10	6	8	3
Female 0	5	Female 0	31,000					
ditto	do.	Male 204	5,600	4	10	6	8	3
		Female 0	13,000					
ditto	do.	Male 207	8,000 16,000	5	10	6	8	3
		Female 0	16,000					
ditto	do.	ditto	ditto	5½	13	6	8	3
2 6-pdr.	7 3 manned simulta- neously	208	13,000	5½	14	6	8	3
—	2	—	5,400	9	7	4	3	3
—	3	—	7,500	6½	8	4	4	3
Male 16-pdr.	2	Male 100	5,400	8	9	4	4	3
Female 0	3	Female 0	7,200					

EQUIPMENT.

1 3-pdr.	2 M.G.	90	5,000	20	6	3	5	3
—	one .5" one .303"	—	2,500	45	—	—	3 or 4	2.5
—	—	—	—	33	—	—	—	1.5
—	—	—	—	27	—	—	—	2

:, nor can a figure be given for the cross-country speed. The lowest
p to a 45 degree slope, but wheel or track slip generally occurs before

can travel on one fill.
S.A.A. on all vital parts.
scribed in Chapters XVI. and XVII. They are too experimental at

INDEX.

	PAGE.
Air Co-operation	37, 161, 171
Air Compressor Plant	143
American Tank Corps	39
Amiens, Battle of	30, 37
Anley, Gen.	19
Anti-tank Gun	177
Armoured Brigade, Medium	216
Armoured Brigade, Light	216
Armoured Cars	212
Armoured Carriers	201
Armoured Fighting Vehicles, Classification of	201
Armoured Force	93, 98, 147
Armoured Machine Gun Carriers	230
Arras, Battle of, First	19
Arras, Battle of, Second	35
Artillery, Director of	180
Austin Scout	240, 242
Baker-Carr, Brig.-Gen., C. D'A. B. S.	29
Bapaume, Battle of	34, 37
Bateman, Lt.-Col. H. H.	137, 138
Bermicourt	15, 28, 66
Box Girder Bridge	133
Broad, Col. C. N. F.	99
Burnett Stuart, Gen. Sir John	219, 226
Cable Suspension for Tanks	76
Cambrai, Battle of, 11, 21 et seq.	
Canal Lock Bridge	126
Capper, General Sir John	19, 99
Carden Loyd Tank	119-122
Carriemore Trailer	141
Carter, Lt.-Col. E. J.	37
Churchill, Rt. Hon. Winston	5
Christchurch	78, 128
Collins, Brig. R. J.	148, 154
Courage, Brig.-Gen. A.	29
Crossley Lorry	101
Davies, Capt. R. D.	145
Dragon	92

	PAGE.
Elles, Gen. Sir H. J.,	14, 19, 36, 98
Elverdon	6
Epehy, Battle of	35
Epicyclic Speed Gear	42
Field Company R.E. 17th,	138 et seq.
Foot, Maj. S. H.	54
Ford, Henry	187
Fowler Plough for Trench Cutting	132
Fuller, Maj.-Gen. J. F. C.,	3, 7, 16, 31, 69, 71, 92
Gallieni, General	238
Glasgow, Brig.-Gen. W.	36
Haig, Earl	8
Hankey, Brig.-Gen. C. G.	98
Hathi Tractor	100
Heavy Branch M.G.C.	6, 14
Hotblack, Capt. F. E.	14
India	246
Infighters	232
Inglis, Maj. (Professor) C. E.	127, 128
Inglis Tubular Bridge	128, 129
Johnson, Lt. Col. P., 45, 75, 77, 83, 90, 108	
Karslake, Brig. H.	31, 110
Kegresse Track	101
Laird, Brig. K. M.	99
Laryngaphone	70
Liberty Tank and Engine	41
Liddell Hart, Capt. B. H.	114, 149
Light Box Girder Bridge	145
Lindsay, Brig.-Gen. G. M.	98
Lloyd, Brig.-Gen. Hardress	29
Locarno Pact	4, 243
Ludendorf, Gen.	34
Mallory, Major T.	37
Mat Bridge	142
Maubeuge	85
Mechanical Warfare Board	181

Mechanization, Directorate of	181, 203
Messines, Battle of	20
Military College of Science	184, 192
Milne, F.-M. Sir George	125, 154
Ministry of Munitions,	10, 11, 26, 65
Minesweeping Rollers	131
Mines, Anti-tank	135, 172
Mobility of Tanks	208
Montgomery-Massingberd, Gen. Sir A. A.	169
Mole Draining Plough	132
Morris Commercial Lorry,	101 et seq.
Morris, Sir William	187
Morris Tank	120-122
National Phys. Laboratory	193
One-Man Tank	114
Ordnance Mech. Engrs.	188-191
Pavesi Tractor	104
Penn, O. S.	110
Pile, Col. F. A.	148
Pontoon Bridge	166
Pontoon Equipment	135
Pontoon Transport	148
Renault Tank	26
R.E. Board	138
Repair Work	182
Research Work	193-196
R.E. Tank	130
Ricardo Engine	27
Roadless Traction	247-248
Road Train	108
R.A.S.C., 58, et seq.,	100, 182
Royal Engineers	190
Royal Navy	249
St. Quentin, Battle of	35
Salvage Companies	66
Searle, Col. F.	60, 67
Selle, Battle of	85
Signal Coy. for Tanks	157
Six-wheel Lorry	102
Sledges	58
Smoke	50, 236
Sponsons	5
Stern, Sir A.	5
Supply Tanks	53, 54
Swimming Tanks	75, 212
Swinton, Gen. Sir E. O.	5, 6, 11, 19
Tank Economics	56, 57
Tanks, Close Support	210
Tanks, Heavy	24, 203
Tanks, Light	25, 207
Tanks, Medium	24, 204
Tanks, Mark I	5, 16
Tanks, Mark V	26, 31
Tanks, Mark VIII	41, 73
Tanks, Medium A	24, 31
Tanks, Medium C	43, 73
Tanks, Medium D	72, 73, 82
Tanks, One-man	114
Tank, Stepping Stones	141
Tank, Vickers Mark I	91
Tank, Vickers Mark II	91, 97
Transmission, Petrol-Electric	42
Transport, First Line	238
Trestle for Bridging	135
Unditching Beam	49
Uzielli, Col. T. J.	14
Villers-Bretonneux, Battle of	30
Yarnbury Castle	162
Wakeley, A. V. T., Maj.	138
Whippet Tank	24
William Janney Speed Gear	41
Wilson, Maj.	18, 42
Wireless	159
Wool	98

www.ingramcontent.com/pod-product-compliance
Lightning Source LLC
Chambersburg PA
CBHW071812230426
43670CB00013B/2434